The Famine in Mayo

1845 – 1850

A Portrait from Contemporary Sources

Compiled and Edited by
IVOR HAMROCK

MAYO COUNTY COUNCIL
1998

First Published 1998.

MAYO COUNTY COUNCIL
Aras an Chontae,
Castlebar,
County Mayo,
Ireland.

© Mayo County Council.

All rights reserved.
No part of this publication may be reproduced or transmitted in any form
without the permission of the publisher.

ISBN: 0 951962426

Printed by: The Western People.

Contents

Foreword

THE Great Famine was one of the defining moments of Irish history. It marked a watershed in the history of the country causing a change so complete in the Irish social and political circumstances, that the fabric of the peoples sensibilities would never be the same again. No longer could the Irish people trust to the land to provide constant sustenance. No longer could they rely on what security of tenure that the landlords allowed them, and most importantly they learned that their English political masters cared little for their plight.

Yet for many years the Famine was ignored in academic circles. It was only as the 150th anniversary of this tragic event was being commemorated that the huge effort that the Famine had on Irish social and cultural history began to be acknowledged. In 1996, as part of Mayo County Council's contribution to these commemorations, a major exhibition was produced by the County Library Service. The material for the exhibition was drawn entirely from contemporary sources – eyewitness accounts, official records and reports in local newspapers of the period and was illustrated with prints, photographs and maps. Researched and compiled by Ivor Hamrock, Senior Library Assistant, the exhibition toured the county and was also shown in the House of Commons, London. It was widely praised both locally and nationally for its academic content and presentation.

Due to continuing demands from various groups to have the exhibition on loan for display, it was decided to make the material available in book form. Ivor Hamrock edited his original material, assembled it in chapter form and wrote the linking material. The result in a comprehensive picture of Mayo in the Famine years.

This is the first publication by Mayo County Library. It would not have been possible without the dedication of the library staff and in particular the scholarship of Ivor Hamrock. I also wish to thank Mayo County Council for their continued support of the library service through the County Library Advisory Committee.

• Austin Vaughan,
County Library.

Introduction

THE Great Famine of 1845-1849 was the most tragic episode of Irish history. The total dependence of the major proportion of the population on the potato as the source of sustenance had devastating consequences. The destruction of the potato crop by blight resulted in the death of countless people and led to a tide of emigration which would continue down the decades. The population of Ireland in 1841 had risen to over 8 million, but by 1851, it fell to 6.5m. In that period the population of County Mayo declined by 29 per cent from 388,887 to 247,830. Deaths and emigration accounted for the loss of 114,057 of Mayo's population – a stark figure when compared to the county's population today of 111,524 (1996 census).

Many historians have documented and analysed the Famine and the politics and economy of the period has been the subject of many books. This book is not intended as such a study. It is a portrait of the lives and deaths of the people as recorded by witnesses in books, newspapers and official records of that period.

These articles are reproduced as they appeared originally except in some cases where portions of lengthy passages have been omitted. The spellings of placenames are also as in the original. The introduction to each chapter and the headings of articles are the work of the compiler and are only intended as an aid to the reader.

The Potato Disease

The first reports of blight appeared in September of 1845. For one third of the country's population of eight million, the nutritious lumper potato was the sole article of diet. In County Mayo, it was estimated that nine tenths of the population depended on it. An acre and a half of land could provide enough potatoes to support a family for most of the year. Any other crops or animals the smallholder raised went to pay rent. A potato famine was a great calamity.

THE POTATO CROP

Mayo Constitution 11-11-1845

On this subject we have little more to add to what we said in our last number. In some cases the damage is found, on digging out the potatoes, to be only partial, in other cases the injury and loss are, very great. However, if the disease could be arrested after digging the damage would not be so extensive as to give cause for the apprehensions entertained. But if unhappily the disease spread, after the potatoes are pitted, to anything like the extent we have heard of in some cases, the consequences would be frightful. Last week large quantities of damaged potatoes were sent into the market, the owners wishing to get rid of them as soon as possible. The consequences was that the price was comparatively low. It has risen since then, however,

and on Saturday it was from 2.5d. to 3d per stone. The price of oats remains stationary, at from 6s.4d. to 6s.6d.

CROPS LOST

Mayo Constitution 25-11-1845

Large quantities of potatoes that have been pitted sound have, on examination afterwards, been found unfit for use. So general is this that we have heard some gentlemen of experience, and who are well acquainted with the state of the crops in their districts, say that they greatly fear there will hardly be a sound potato in the country in a month of two. The Earl of Lucan states that he has lost one-half his crop, and when he has lost so much, or when his potatoes have been so much damaged, with the utmost care that has been bestowed on them, and the adoption of every

conceivable remedy, how must the potatoes of the people throughout the country be, when they can scarcely be said to adopt any remedy at all? They are in general pitting them in the usual way, except that they are, at least in some places, making the pits smaller. Some of the poor law guardians stated at the meeting of the board on Saturday that they thought about one-half the crop was lost. If so, even with the good return that has been this year, there would be great danger of a scarcity, unless the grain be kept in the country. And how are the persons who have not a sufficiency of grain to obtain it, unless they get employment? In some cases the people, seeing the destruction of the potatoes in the pits, are leaving them in the ground, in the hope that they will be safer there than if dug and placed in pits or

The discovery of the blight.

together, and we have heard of some cases where the disease had made such progress that the crop was abandoned altogether, as not worth being dug, or the trouble of attempting to save any of it.

season, at low prices, which is now paying for its storage nearly cent per cent – in proof whereof we refer our readers to the following table of prices for Castlebar for the months of October, 1844 and 1845:–

potato crop, I, as a subscriber to your paper, request you will insert therein, and that with confidence as to the fact, that the disease is progressing to an alarming extent, and that two-thirds of the potato crop is lost in the neighbouring villages about me. I had fifty barrels of potatoes this year; I took the strictest care and attention in picking and separating those infected from those I considered sound, and all other possible means of preserving them; but after all my exertions I have not ten barrels out of the entire crop safe. Others of my neighbours left them undug, the crop being totally destroyed. Any person who may doubt this statement can call to me and I will show them ample proof of the facts, at so short a distance as a quarter of a mile from your office.

	1844		1845		Advance	
	s	d	s	d	s	d
Wheat per cwt.	7	6	12	6	5	0
1st Flour ditto	17	0	20	0	3	0
2d ditto ditto	14	0	16	6	2	6
3rd ditto ditto	10	0	14	6	4	6
Oats per ditto	4	6	7	6	3	0
Oatmeal ditto ditto	9	2	16	6	7	4
Bran per cwt.	4	6	8	0	3	6

I am, Sir, yours truly,

THOMAS DAVIS.

THE POTATO DISEASE – AND ITS EFFECTS ON OUR MARKETS

The Telegraph (29-11-1845)

It is with great regret we are compelled to acknowledge that the reports of last week, regarding the disease in the potatoes throughout this county, are but too true. We have seen some of those affected by the disease – to a casual observer they would appear perfectly sound – but upon a close examination of that part of the potato attached to the stem, we found them of a dark hue, and on the least pressure of the finger the water oozed out, having a sour smell – exactly like that of frosted potatoes.

Through all parts of the county the alarm has been spread. The consequences is that the prices of oats, oatmeal, wheat, flour, bran, etc., have risen to an alarming pitch at this early season of the year, and if the panic, thus created by so calamitous a visitation, be not speedily checked, what will become of the poor? We, notwithstanding that there is a partial failure in the poor man's staff of life, believe that abundance of provisions will still remain, if not carried out of the country by speculators, who, disregarding the poor, seek their own aggrandisement – many of them having oats and wheat laid by since last

– At Ballyvary Mills, we have been told, the price is 44s per bag, or 22s per cwt.

– The price demanded at Mr. MacDonnell's Store in this town.

Landlords of Mayo, look upon the foregoing table, and ask yourself – "What is to be done?" We iterate our former opinion, that there will be plenty of food, in the country if properly managed. Remember, gentlemen, you are the guardians of your tenantry. Remember also that there are ten months to come before the people can again have recourse to a fresh supply from the earth. Remember likewise, if this high price be allowed to advance, that your tenantry will not (with very few exceptions, indeed), be able to make a tillage in the next Spring – and then, what is to become of our numerous population? The contemplation is sickening to every humane heart. And how can you expect your rack-rents to be paid?

THE POTATO CROP TO THE EDITOR OF THE CONSTITUTION

Rathbane,
29th December, 1845.

Sir – Finding in the last number of your paper an article relative to the condition of the

THE POTATO CROP

Mayo Constitution 28-7-1846

It is painful to us to mention that numerous complaints of failures in the potato crop have reached us within the last week. Large fields in the vicinity of this town, which looked luxuriant and healthy a month since, are now altogether black and withered. The oat and barley crops do not now promise as well as was anticipated; and in some instances, it is said, even the fruit trees have suffered by the blight. On this important subject the Tyrawly Herald says:

"We regret that the appearance of the potato crop has given us no cause to alter for the better our remarks last week. Whatever may be the intention of the small farmers, or however they may regard the appearance of the disease in the new crop, they do not seem to be much alarmed."

THE POTATO DISEASE

Mayo Constitution 4-8-1846.

We have been much alarmed during the past week at the fearful accounts of the potato crop. The work of destruction is going rapidly forward on every side of us. – Within the last week large quantities of the tubers have become blackened, and the potatoes, when dug, are quite infected. The crops which a few days since were apparently safe, have, on investigation, been found diseased. "We heard several of the guardians at the last poor law meeting state, that the stench arising from the potato fields during the night was insufferable. The disease presents the same appearance as that of last year, except that decomposition is taking place much more rapidly, so much so that we fear is a great part of the crop is already lost. Several farmers in the neighbourhood of this town sent early potatoes to the market which, when sold, appeared sound, but on being boiled were unfit for food. We have heard very distressing accounts from our Ballinrobe, Newport, Westport and Ballina correspondents. The oat and wheat crops look very healthy, and promise an abundant return. We are happy to say that much more grain has been sown in this neighbourhood this year than for many preceding years.

WITHERED AWAY

The Telegraph 5-8-1846

The dreadful reality is beyond yea or nay in this county. From one end to the other the weal has gone forth that the rot is increasing with fearful rapidity. From our own personal knowledge, as well as the reports we have

The Village of Dooagh, Achill

received from the rural districts, we regret to say no description of potatoes have escaped – late as well as early planting are rapidly decomposing. Many persons are digging them out to make room for winter crops. We regret to say that a blight has also come on the oat crop: in many fields around this town, one-third at least, has been already rendered useless by smut. During last week a report prevailed that the rooks were all dying in the fields and rookeries. The dew on last Friday night has done immense damage to the growing crops. The potato tops have been nearly all withered away by it, and several persons have declared to us that they had put some of this dew on their tongues to try if it were honey: it proved, however, very bitter and many found it to emit a disagreeable smell. About eight days past a shower of rain fell which discoloured the clothes bleaching in a garden in this town, and much difficulty was experienced in removing the black stains occasioned by it. The alarm of the people, both rich and poor, is very great. One thing is certain, the staple food of the people is gone: and the Government cannot too soon exert themselves to make provision to provide against certain famine.

PERSECUTION AND STARVATION

The Telegraph 19-8-1846.

On Monday last upwards of 500 poor, wretched, emaciated human beings assembled, with loys, shovels, etc., at Greenhills, the residence of Dominick J. Burke, Esq., J. P., demanding work to keep them from dying of starvation. Their appearance and their declarations before the God of Heaven – to two respectable gentlemen, our informants – that unless speedily relieved, they and their families would be all dead from starvation, elicited much commiseration from all who beheld them. One of those gentlemen declared to us he cried from pity for their sufferings. The poor wretches crowded round the car on which the gentlemen were seated, as if craving their aid, but offering no violence. Noble and generous hearted wretches – their sense of feeling for the hungry children was put to a hard test on that day! Hear it, Englishmen, and say would you act like the men of Islandeady. Five-hundred heads of families were assembled on the Queen's highway, starvation in their countenances – hunger drugging their very vitals asunder –

their wives and children not able to travel from their homes, for want of food. Thus placed and thus circumstanced, two rich merchants, on their way, perhaps from one of the Westport Banks, pass through the crowd unmolested and uninjured. But this is not all – on that day, and while the hungry lamentations of the people were borne aloft to the Throne of Heaven – several car loads of meal or flour passed through without an effort being made to obtain that which would, for a short time, preserve existence. Such noble conduct deserves to be recorded in letters of gold, and speaks volumes for the honour and honesty of our poor countrymen. Yet how long will they be able to act thus? The Landlords are now actually calling for their rents! The drivers are gone forth! – the potatoes are gone before them – The Treasury minute has followed the potatoes – the grain is unripe in the fields – death is now loose! – the green church yards open their graves to receive the victims of persecution and starvation!

We tell the Landlords in the present contingency it is foolishness to talk of law, or to threaten their pauper and starving tenantry with military force. Come what may the people must be fed.

TOTAL FAILURE

Achill Missionary Herald (August, 1846).

The famine of 1846 has now been partially mitigated for a season by the coming-in of the new potato crop. We take this opportunity of thanking the Protestant public for enabling us to relieve the wants not only of our own people, but also of many of our Romish neighbours during the distressing scarcity, and we particularly thank the conductors of the Protestant newspaper press for the kind readiness with which they publish our appeals to Protestant liberality. We are sorry to inform

GUANO: An imported fertiliser suspected of carrying blight.

our readers that the relief offered by the growing crops is very partial and temporary. The potato crop, on which the people depended for their support for the coming year, has proved in many cases a total failure, and taking a general view of its deficiency, we are persuaded that it will not suffice to maintain the population of this island for much more than two months. We believe that by the first of November there will hardly be a potato in the island, and then ten long months of famine are before us. To meet such a disastrous state of things, whatever efforts may be made by the government, they will need to be aided, and aided largely, by private and individual liberality.

PETITION TO BRITISH PRIME MINISTER

The Telegraph 26-8-1846.

To the Right Hon. Lord John Russell, First Lord of the Treasury, etc.

"My Lord – We, the

inhabitants of the parishes of Anglish, Ballyhean, Breaffy, Turlough, Islandeady, Touaghty, Drum, Rosslee, Ballintubber, Barriscarra, Kilmeena and Kilmaclasser, in the county of Mayo, in public meeting assembled in the open air, on the Green of Castlebar, beg leave respectfully to submit to you that in consequences of the total failure of the potato crop of the present season, in addition to the partial loss of that crop in the last season, the great bulk of the people of these parishes, and of the county generally, are reduced to a state of utmost destitution, and that starvation with all its horrors must immediately ensue, and the people will, unless relieved, inevitably perish by hundreds and thousands.

"Under such appaling circumstances, your petitioners call upon you, as the First Minister of the greatest empire in the world, to take such steps as will avert the threatened calamity.

"Your petitioners beg to state, that partial measures of relief such as had been adopted by the Government during the late destitution, will be totally insufficient to meet the present awful calamity, which has befallen, in the loss of the ordinary food of the great majority of the people of Ireland.

"Petitioners beg also to submit that should it be the will of the Government that relief be extended through the medium of employment upon public works, a better system than that hitherto existing should be adopted, so as to give prompt payment to the labourers, instead of subjecting them, as at present, to the loss of many journeys and several days in seeking payment of their laird-earned wages.

"Signed on behalf of the meeting, consisting of at least Twenty Thousand persons.

Richard S. Bourke, *Chairman;*
James Conry, *Secretary.*

TREATMENT OF DISEASED POTATOES

Mayo Constitution (8-9-1846).

Mr. W. Herbert Saunders, in a letter to the editor of the Cork Constitution on this subject, notices the statement of a "Windsor farmer," "that he left, last year a field of distressed potatoes in the ground to rot as manure, but that in eighteen months after, when he dug up the ground, he found them all sound, to his great surprise."

Mr. Saunders says he does not believe in this wholesale metamorphosis, but recommends that the branches of stalks of all blighted potato fields should be pulled up, and added to the dunghill, provided that the potatoes are at the time in a state worth preserving. We take the following paragraph from the letter of Mr. Saunders:–

"In every case where the quantity of sound potatoes in a Blighted field is worth preserving, place both your feet at each side of the blighted stalk and pull them up, hardening the holes with the soles of your

Searching for potatoes.

shoes as you proceed, and dig out your potatoes as you want them for daily use, separating the bad for the pigs. the rationale of this is as follows. When left in the ground the very decayed potatoes rot without infecting the sound, for they are not in "juxta position," and you remove the communication of wet and taint, by removing the blighted stalks, which act as conductors to wet and infection; for when you pull up a blighted stalk, the decayed shoot leading to the decaying potato comes away with the stalk, leaving all the wholesome shoots in the ground. If you can spare the use of ground, there is no better way to "pit" your potatoes in order to preserve them than by leaving them in the ground as above recommended, and this fact has been proved in several instances."

- Freeman.

The Hungry Years

The damage done by the blight in 1845 was only partial and most people had enough to get through the winter. Government relief anf local charity also helped. The year 1846 brought disaster as the blight destroyed most of the crop. Overnight, fields of promising green stalks blackened and the tubers below turned to mush. In 1847, after two successive years of blight, many chose to eat whatever seed they had, rather than risk planting. There was no blight in that year, but there were no crops either. Black '47 saw the advent of fevers such as typhus, which rapidly spread through the weakened population.

WESTPORT

The Telegraph (26-8-1846).

On Saturday last the inhabitants of Westport witnessed a novel, and at the same time, a heart-rendering sight. About mid-day some thousands of the rural population marched into town to have an interview with the Most Noble the Marquis of Sligo: they approached the grand entrance of the Noble Lord's residence, and having, after some little delay, obtained admittance, they proceeded, with the most becoming order to the Castle, none attempting to even walk off the road, lest their doing so might injure the grass of the demesne. Having arrived before the hall door the Noble Marquis (as was custom of his deceased father) instantly came forward to meet them: he talked with them: deplored the visitation with which God had affiliated the land: told them he would instantly state their condition to the Government, in order to obtain them relief, and that as to

himself, he would go as far as any landlord in the country to redress the grievances of his tenantry. He also told them that his intention was not to harass them with regard to his rents: that then it was almost useless to talk on that subject, as the time for collecting the rent had not yet arrived. Finally, the Noble Marquis assured them that no exertions of his should be spared to obtain for them, from Her Majesty's Government immediate employment. The people expressed themselves satisfied with the declarations of their Noble Landlord and returned to the town in the same orderly manner which characterised their march to the castle.

MASSBROOK

Mayo Constitution (27-8-1846).

On last Tuesday night the dead body of a man named Anthony Donnelly, who lived near Massbrook, in the parish of Adrigoole, was found on the mountains about a mile distant

from his residence. It appeared from the evidence of some members of his family, at the inquest, that their food for the previous week was nothing better than rotten potatoes, and that he went on the day before his body was found to Castlebar to purchase some trifling articles for a few pence, the only money in his possession. It is stated that Donnelly was employed for eight or ten days on the public works, but was stopped a week before his death and had not since received any payment. The Coroner's jury found a verdict, that deceased came by his death in consequence of the want of a sufficient supply of food.

FOXFORD

The Telegraph (23-9-1846).

One misfortun brings another. – We regret to state that fever, to an alarming extent has, at length, made its appearance in this county. Our Foxford Correspondent states, that never, in his memory, was fever so prevalent in that locality as at present. In the villages between that town and the Pontoon, entire families are lying, and many dying. He mentions one family in particular, eight of whom are confined to the bed of sickness, their only attendant being a boy six years old! Several other families have no person to wet their parched lips, the neighbours being in dread to approach the cabins of contagion. The scourge has now gone forth, and what may be spared by one calamity will, we fear, be

A village in famine times.

hurried off by another. – Such is the situation of the poor while the rich are making no effort, by friendly contributions, to relieve the necessities of the people, whose sinewy arms enabled them to fare sumptuously every day. Now they are lying low and their moans unheeded, save by the carrion crow, who, perched aloft upon the top of some lofty oak, croakes on the dying knell of many hapless victims of fever and starvation. God of mercy, receive their souls into thy glorious kingdom. May their transit from this world be a happy one.

CASTLEBAR

The Telegraph (6-10-1846).

In the neighbourhood of Castlebar, we have heard of parents putting their children to bed to sleep off the hunger which was gnawing their hearts. Nay, we have talked with a poor woman a few days since who told us that she had left four children at home in bed – that for the two days previously they had not tasted food – on that day she earned a few pence, by carrying out turf on her back from the bog to the road side – that she undertook this laborious work, on a weak and empty stomach – that she might get even one stone of potatoes for her poor children. Does the statement of this wretched woman need comment?

CONG

The Telegraph (6-10-1846).

The accounts which have reached us from all parts of Ireland since our last publication, regarding the sufferings of the poor, are truly heart-rending. We read of parents dying from want of food – children, unconscious of the extent of their misery, standing at the bedside of their lifeless parent calling to him for something to appease their hunger – they call in vain – hunger has snatched to another,

and a better world, their prop and and mainstay. This reader, is no fiction, it has occurred at Dungarvan.

But why should we look for such proof of want elsewhere when we can be supplied with abundance of them in our own country? The Rev. Mr. Waldron, P.P. of Cong, states that three of his unhappy parishioners have paid the debt of nature from the pressure of distress, and this in a county where abundance of provisions is said to exist. – From the same place the respected Protestant Rector, the Rev. Mr. Moore, has again forwarded a memorial to the Lord Lieutenant, which we publish elsewhere, giving a most appaling description of the state to which his parishioners are reduced and calling upon the Government to act with promptitude. The Dublin Evening Mail, in the most unbecoming and uncalled for manner treats the statement of Mr. Moore, as a well conceived fiction. Alas! little does the editor know the wants and sufferings of the poor in Mayo.

BALLINA

Tyrawly Herald (26-11-1846).

An inquest was held in this town, on Tuesday last, by Mr. Atkinson, Coroner, on the body of Hugh Daly. After the examination of witnesses, amongst whom was the medical gentleman, Dr. Whittaker, who examined the body, the jury found that the deceased came by his death in consequence of insufficiency of food.

BALLYCASTLE

Tyrawly Herald (29-10-1846).

We regret to state that on Tuesday last, a worker, named Bridget Thomash, died of actual starvation within a short distance of Ballycastle. It was sworn to at the Inquest that she had not partaken of more than one scanty meal per day, for the

last fortnight, and on some occasions she had nothing whatever to support nature. There are hundreds of poor creatures in the same locality who are similarly circumstanced, and if immediate relief is not afforded they, too, shall meet with the same dreadful death.

PALMERSTOWN

Tyrawly Herald (12-11-1846).

On Friday morning last a woman named Melody died of starvation near Palmerstown. The unfortunate creature procured shelter during the previous night in the cabin of another poor woman, and while there drank a mixture of a very small quantity of meal she had with her and some water. She slept on some straw, and in the morning when she made an effort to get up she fell from exhaustion and died shortly afterwards. Surgeons, Neilson and Townley, who made a post mortem examination at the Inquest, deposed that her death was caused by insufficiency of food. They found that her stomach, which was greatly contracted in size, contained only about two tablespoonfuls of fluid, and that there was no food whatever in the large intestine. The heart was extremely small, and there were some traces of inflammation in the stomach. A verdict was returned by the jury in accordance with the medical evidence.

CROSSMOLINA

Tyrawly Herald (10-12-1846).

On Thursday last, Mr. Atkinson, Coroner, held an inquest at Crossmolina on the body of man named Martin M'Gever. The jury found a verdict of death from want of sufficient food.

On Saturday, Mr. Atkinson held an inquest on the body of John Barrett, at Cloomalogh near Killala. Several witnesses were examined who, with Dr.

Neilson, who examined the body, stated that the deceased came by his death in consequence of insufficiency of food.

On Sunday, the same Coroner inquired into the cause of the death of Anthony Malley, at Notlish, in the vicinity of Crossmolina. Dr. McNair, who made a post mortem examination concurred with the witnesses, that death was caused by starvation.

On the same day, Mr. Atkinson held an inquest on the body of John Munnelly, at Ballymoholy. After the examination of witnesses and the medical attendant a similar verdict to the foregoing was returned.

LACKEN

**Mayo Constitution
(22-12-1846).**

On Friday the same coroner held an inquest on the body of John Ruane of Lacken. Deceased was found on Thursday, by a little girl, near the chapel of Lacken, lying dead on the footpath. He belongs to a colony of fishermen, who were comfortable in their own way, before the present calamity, but are now scattered throughout the country. The jury returned a verdict of death from starvation.

ROBEEN

**Mayo Constitution
(22-12-1846).**

MORE STARVATION – On the 16th instant, Mr. Rutledge, coroner, held an inquest at Robin, on the body of Catherine Walsh, who died of absolute starvation. One of the witnesses deposed that the deceased was able to work on the roads until the inclement weather set in, when, from her age, she was unable to withstand the cold, and therefore she could not procure food. Dr. Little declared the cause of her death to be from the absolute want of the necessaries of life.

1846!

Would that we could say farewell! But that is impossible: we are groaning with anguish: we are palled at the wreck thou hast made. We could curse three – but no – you are gone: and we fight not with shadows.

1847

You have found unsubdued: you have found us crushed down by starvation, disease, and death: be it thy happy destiny to change this order of things: to stay the ravages of famine: to throw over the troubled earth the cornucopia: to cheer the drooping, bereaved, and the broken hearted: to cause the soil of our lovely country to reward the toil of the husbandman with plenty of food for the use of God's creatures. In your career may peace and happiness accompany you: and may our rulers, even in this thy day, take wise counsel, and see that it is their solemn and bounden duty to protect, by every means they can command, the lives of Her Majesty's subjects: this they must do if they desire the peace and prosperity of this country, and the stability of the British Throne. Buoyed up with this hope we bid thee, 1847! a thousand welcomes! and may our adieu at your departure, by our bettered condition, be words of regret for your short stay.

The Telegraph (16-1-1847).

CROSSMOLINA
**Mayo Constitution
(22-12-1846).**

On Tuesday last, Mr. Atkinson, Coroner, held an inquest at Crossmolina, on the body of Bernard Regan, son of a butcher, who was in the employment of Messrs. Russell of Limerick. Being out of employment, and having been refused admittance there, he made his way to Galway – together with his seven children – where they were also denied poorhouse relief. They then begged their way to Crossmolina, where the boy died. After the examination of Dr. McNair, and the father and mother of deceased the jury returned a verdict that death was caused by want of food.

WESTPORT

The Telegraph (13-1-1847).

APPALING – The following communication we have received from a Westport correspondent, dated January 8th, 1847: "While walking through the town yesterday, I was asked to go down to the house situated next to the Iron gate (an entrance to the Marquis of Sligo's demesne), and look at the situation of a poor woman who was lying beside her dead husband, a man named Fadgen, a native of Sligo, but the wife belongs to this place. I did go down, and such a deplorable sight I never witnessed. He was lying upon a pallet of straw and the poor wife beside him with her thigh bone out of joint and her leg much swollen. The man's face was fearful to look at, the rats having disfigured it much during the night. A coffin was made which was paid for by Mr. Hildebrand, Captain Higgins and Mr. Levingston. This poor man was interred by the Scavengers, and I have no doubt his death was caused by hunger, and that many such cases are of daily occurrence in this town."

MAYO ABBEY

**Mayo Constitution
(12-1-1847).**

SHOCKING We have been informed that a poor man, at

Mayo, near Balla, after having been reduced to the greatest destitution, was obliged to leave his home to beg, leaving his wife, a feeble old woman, after him. In a few days after his departure some of the neighbours went to the wretched hovel of the old woman, and found her lying on a litter of straw in the corner, with the flesh of her shrivelled arms and face mangled and eat by rats! The wretched creature died in a short time after.

ATTYMASS

Tyrawly Herald (18-2-1847).

Owing to the indisposition of Mr. Atkinson, the Coroner for this district, we are unable to give a list of the number of deaths from starvation, which occurred in this neighbourhood during the past week; but we are informed by a gentleman from Attymass, a parish within three of four miles of this town, that between Friday and Tuesday last, no fewer than eleven persons died from starvation in that locality. When such has been the number there we may imagine

what it must have been throughout the entire district of the coroner. A heavy and an extraordinary visitation is upon the poor people of this country. When shall they receive permanent relief?

BELMULLET

W. J. Bennett (16-3-1847).

We entered a cabin. Stretched in one dark corner, scarcely visible, from the smoke and rags that covered them, were three children huddled together, lying there because they were too weak to rise, pale and ghastly, their little limbs - on removing a portion of the filthy covering – perfectly emaciated, eyes sunk, voice gone, and evidently in the last stage of actual starvation. Crouched over the turf embers was another form, wild and all but naked, scarcely human in appearance. It stirred not, nor noticed us. On some straw, soddened upon the ground, moaning piteously, was a shrivelled old woman, imploring us to give her something – baring her limbs partly, to show how the

skin hung loose from the bones, as soon as she attracted our attention. Above her, on something like a ledge, was a young woman, with sunken cheeks – a mother, I have no doubt – who scarcely raised her eyes in answer to our enquiries, but pressed her hand upon her forehead, with a look of unutterable anguish and despair.

BALLYCROY

Asenath Nicholson (1847).

A visit to the national school gave not a very favourable impression of the state of the children; nearly a hundred pale-faced and bare-footed little ones were crowded into a cold room, squatting upon their feet, cowering closely together, waiting for ten ounces of bread, which was all their support, but now and then a straggling turnip-top. The teacher, with a salary of £12 a year, could not be expected to be of the nicer sort, nor of the highest attainments in education. The improvement of the children would not in some time fit them for a class in college.

Famine
Victims

A view of Castlebar from Knockthomas. *(Wynne Collection).*

CASTLEBAR

The Telegraph (31-3-1847).

"On last Sabbath day while walking in company with a young man from your office, and by my own son, through Gallowshill, in this town, my attention was drawn to a cabin into which we three entered: at the fire was sitting a poor man in an exhausted state from hunger, almost naked, with a child in his arms, the picture of death, sucking the father's fingers as if they were the mother's breast. In an opposite corner stood what answered as a bed, in which were three children lying, with no covering save a fold of an old sooty blanket or sheet. Those children might be aged from six to fourteen years, but from their haggard appearance I cannot be certain as to the probable age of the elder girl – the poor creatures had lost their hair from famine. I involuntarily shrunk back, dreading I was standing in the midst of fever, but being assured there was no danger I asked the half-dead creatures where the mother was, and was told she was out begging with two other little ones who were not as weak as those in the bed. The father said he was after a long attack of sickness which deprived the family of his work on the roads, and that those in the bed were endeavouring to sleep away the gnawings of hunger, not having for two days previously as much food for the

The poor children presented the most piteous and heart-rendering spectacle.

eight as would suffice for one! and that they could not command the price of the soup. I promised to send some relief to the poor victims – and by doing so a fresh claimant attacked me for aid – a poor man with four children and a sick wife: his case was equally bad, for he had been out begging all the morning, without success. In reply to my question he said he would not be admitted in the Poor House without his wife, and she was so sick and weak from want, he could not remove her. Here was a cabin with fourteen skeletons of human beings on the Lord's Day without a fire – without a mouthful of food, and without as much clothes as would cover one out of the fourteen.

KILCOMMON ERRIS

W. J. Bennett (16-3-1847).

Perhaps the poor children presented the most piteous and heart-rendering spectacle. Many were too weak to stand, their little limbs attenuated – except where the frightful swellings had taken the place of previous emaciation – beyond the power of volition when moved. Every infantile expression entirely departed; and in some, reason and intelligence had envidently flown. Many were remnants of families, crowded together in one cabin; orphaned little relatives taken in by the equally destitute, and even strangers, for these poor people are kind to one another to the end. In one cabin was a sister, just dying, lying by the side of her little brother, just dead. I have worse than this to relate, but it is useless to multiply details, and they are, in fact, unfit. They did but rarely complain. When inquired of, what was the matter, the answer was alike in all – "Tha shein ukrosh" – indeed, the hunger. We truly learned the terrible meaning of that sad word "ukrosh." There were many touching incidents.

INVER

Tyrawly Herald (27-5-1847).

In some of the remote parts of this Union, particularly in the barony of Erris, disease is committing serious havoc. On Monday, the 17th inst., in the townland of Inver, in the barony referred to, there were no less than thirty-two human beings dead - dead of famine – dead of pestilence produced and propagated by want. The deaths in this district, arising from destitution and its consequences, are awfully numerous, and of daily occurrence. Even sudden deaths are now of almost momentary frequency, so worn and exhausted are the physical energies of the poor people. On Tuesday last a wretched man dropped dead at Crosspatrick, near Killala, from mere destitution. This is a fearful state of things and what renders it doubly so is its pervading generality.

ERRIS

Asenath Nicholson (1847).

When I went over desolate Erris, and saw the demolished

Newport, County Mayo. c.1840.

cabins belonging to J. Walshe, I begged to know if all had died from that hamlet – "Worse than died," was the answer; for if they are alive, they are in sand banks on the bleak sea-shore, or crowded into some miserable cabin for a night or two, waiting for death; they are lingering out the last hours of suffering.

NEWPORT

Asenath Nicholson (1847).

I found here, at Newport, misery without a mask; the door and window of the kind Mrs. Arthur wore a spectacle of distress indescribable; naked, cold and dying, standing like petrified statues at the window, or imploring, for God's sake, a little food, till I almost wished that I might flee into the wilderness, far, far from the abode of any living creature.

Mrs. Arthur said: 'I have one case to place before you, and will leave all the rest to your own discretion. I have fed a little boy, once a day, whose parents and brothers and sisters are dead, with the exception of one little sister. The boy is seven-years-old, the sister five. They were told they must make application to the poorhouse, at Castlebar, which was ten Irish

miles away. One cold rainy day in November, this boy took his little sister by the hand, and faint with hunger, set off for Castlebar. And now, reader, if you will, follow these little bare-footed, bare-headed Connaught orphans through a muddy road of ten miles, in a rainy day, without food, and see them at the workhouse, late at night. The doors are closed – at last, they succeed in being heard. The girl is received, the boy sent away – no room for him – he made his way back to Newport the next morning, and had lived by crawling into any place he could at night, and once a day called at the door of my friend who fed him.

ISLANDEADY

The Telegraph (20-10-1847).

STARVATION – On Thursday morning last a poor, but once comfortable and respectable man named Patt Henry, of Tovneena, in the parish of Islandeady, with his daughter, died from the effects of hunger. He has left a wife and five children, who will, we fear, soon follow him from the same cause. On the previous day the poor man was seen aboard thro' the village, and it was only after the

Dooagh, Achill, in the 1840s

decease of Henry and his daughter that the neighbours ascertained the extent of the want and misery of this once happy family.

ACHILL

Achill Missionary, Herald, February 1847.

We are sorry to report that the famine increases in intensity in this island. Whatever little resources the natives had are now entirely consumed and they are wholly dependant on the imported supplies of food and the money which they can earn to purchase it. The distress in some of the villages is so great that the poor are endeavouring to maintain themselves on the limpets which they gather on the rocks, and boiled sea weed. During the last month we gave employment to 2,192 labourers, of whom 740 were Roman Catholics, and 1,452 Protestants. This aggregate number gives an average of 100 men per day. The feeding of the 600 children, mentioned in our last, was partially suspended for some time, as our supply of Indian-meal was consumed, but on our being allowed the privilege of purchasing at the government store, the charitable work was resumed.

A small sloop, the Expedition of Milford, freighted with 60 tons of food and different kinds of seed, sailed from the port of Dublin for Achill, on Thursday, the 18th inst. We thank our friends for their liberality in enabling us to send this second cargo, but we are constrained to inform them that we must still draw largely upon their liberality, as we must greatly increase the number of persons employed on the Mission farms. Unless this is done, and done largely and promptly, the same appalling occurrences which have taken place in Skibbereen will be witnessed in Achill. We must therefore earnestly call upon our kind supporters to use their influence in procuring pecuniary assistance. We regret to say that the markets, and freights and insurances have greatly advanced since we despatched the last cargo, so that the same amount of good cannot be accomplished with the same sum of money which might have sufficed some months ago.

We have also to report the appearance of both fever and dysentery in the island. One of our settlers, the mother of a large family, fell a victim to the former. God only knows what suffering is to be endured before the harvest of this year comes in. Were not our trust in Him we should be overwhelmed with anxiety, but we know that He can do great and wondrous things which we looked not for.

BEKAN

Mayo Constitution (11-1-1848).

Richard P. O'Grady, Esq., Coroner, held an inquest on the 8th ultimo, on the body of Michael Cunnane, of the parish of Becan. Verdict – "Death from insufficiency of food."

The same Coroner held inquests on the 10th, 11th, 12th and 18th ult., on the bodies of James Cunnane, Winifred Kilgallen, Thomas Kilgallen and Patrick Duffy, when verdicts of death from want, destitution, etc., were found by the same juries.

SHRULE

Mayo Constitution (11-1-1848).

ANOTHER DEATH FROM STARVATION – On Wednesday last, Mr. Ruttledge, Coroner, held an inquest at Shrule, on the body of John Toole, who was found dead on the road side, having been overcome by exhaustion and hunger whilst on his way to beg a morsel of food. The jury after examining several witnesses returned a verdict of "death from starvation." The fearful list of deaths from starvation again threaten to become as horrifying this season as last, with much less hopes of relief; and we trust that some steps will be taken by which to meet the exigencies of the present moment.

CASTLEBAR, KILLASSER, NEWPORT

The Telegraph (16-2-1848).

STARVATION DEATHS! – We are again called upon to record the work of destruction, through want; in our neighbourhood. Our statistical accounts this day must appeal every person possessed of Christian faith:–

No. 1.: A poor woman found dead on the Westport road, left

for days unburied on the side of the road, with a stone at the head and another at the feet. A shocking sight!

No. 2: Thomas Cosgrave, of Lacheel, Parish of Drum.

No. 3: Cosgrave's child.

No. 4: Rose Hoban, of Knocksaxon, parish of Strade: eight days dead before she was interred!

No. 5: John Malley, of Carreenchar, parish of Balla, an orphan boy.

Within the last month in the parish of Killasser, Barony of Gallen, County of Mayo:

No. 6: Joseph Gallagher's wife of Tolligne.

No. 7: Patt Holleran, of Dunmeanor.

No. 8: Patt Holleran's son, of same place.

No. 9: David Moran's daughter, of Cartron.

No. 10: On Monday a poor man dropped dead in the same parish, who was turned out of the workhouse, after his having used many entreaties to be left in the house. After his eviction he only scrambled about three miles from Swinford when he dropped dead on the road.

No. 11: Mrs. Kilcoyne, of Struphane, Castlebar, dysentery, through want.

No. 12: John Duffy, of same street, same complaint, and occasioned by want.

No. 13: A poor person in same street, name not known to us, same complaint, brought on by want.

No. 14: In Barrack Street, a child of Moran's, the Clifden Schoolmaster, died of starvation – the mother and the rest of the children starving since they lost the relief – the husband and father, neglecting to support his family. The Guardians should relieve the wretched creatures and take proceedings against the expounder of the Scriptures in Clifden.

No. 15; A young man in Newport: carried on his old mother's back to the grave, without a coffin! slung by two straw ropes.

No. 16: A boy on the Newport road, so long dead that we are told the body had partly melted away!

No. 17: A poor man, name unknown, was found dead in a village in the parish of Kilmeena, on Saturday last, lying by the side of the ditch; and was exposed there three days before the priest heard of it.

BALLINTUBBER

The Telegraph (23-2-1848).

PARISH OF BALLINTUBBER – Ned Burke, a widow's son (nine in family). The deceased applied to the relieving officer for relief: offered to give up his house and land. The middleman refused the possession. The unfortunate man then went to the agent of the head landlord (Lord Erne): the agent refused to interfere. The man's sufferings at last terminated after lingering on for a whole week nearly without a morsel of food.

Michael Connor, in the same village died from starvation. The deceased also offered his house and land to the landlord, but would get no licence for relief without throwing down his house. After having made several efforts, in vain, between the middleman and the relieving officer, to obtain relief, the unfortunate wretch at last sunk under his sufferings and perished from hunger.

Mary Tuohy, of Greenfield, died from hunger. She held a small cabin, but having refused to throw it down, she was refused a certificate for relief.

John Donelan, of Ballintubber, died of starvation.

Peggy Moran, found dead on the 20th by the ditch side. She applied three times for relief. The third time her name was put on; but she was a corpse when the relief was obtained.

Bridget Colleran, died on the 20th, of hunger.

Anne Tuohy, died on the 20th, of starvation.

James Kyne, of Clonee, Ballintubber, dead by hunger.

Struck down by fever.

Michael Carney, Feebane; Pat Fitzmaurice, Banoryues; Walter Burke, Mellonhill; Anthony Roach, Mellonhill; Michael Joyce, Knockavaha; Thomas Byrne, Knockavaha – Some in the prime of life – the hope and pride of the parish blasted like a young flower.

BALLYHAUNIS

Mayo Constitution (29-2-1848).

The scenes which last year have made our county notorious for sufferings and deaths from starvation, have not, we regret to say, ended with the year 1847. The present season promises to be as fruitful in horrors, without any prospect of such noble interest being taken in our misery, the public being deluded into the impression that out-door relief will or can meet the wants of the people. The following inquests prove the unfortunate condition in which the people are, and, we are sorry to say, they are not a tithe of the cases of "starvation" which are of daily occurrence, and must fearfully increase:–

On the 25th inst., Richard O'Grady, Esq., Coroner, held an inquest at Ballyhaunis, on the body of John Loftus; the jury returned a verdict of "death from starvation and cold."

On the same day, the same Coroner held an inquest on the body of Denis Carroll; verdict – "death from extreme hunger."

LOUISBURGH

Asenath Nicholson (1848).

The little town of Louisburgh, two miles from "Old Head," had suffered extremely. An active priest and faithful protestant curate were doing their utmost to mitigate the suffering, which was like throwing dust in the wind; lost, lost for ever – the work of death goes on, and what is repaired today is broken tomorrow. Many have fallen

A typical cabin at the time of the famine.

under their labours. The graves of the protestant curate and his wife were pointed out to me in the church-yard, who had fallen since the famine, in the excess of their labour; and the present curate and his praiseworthy wife, unless they have supernatural strength, cannot long keep up the dreadful struggle. He employed as many labourers as he could pay, at four-pence a-day, and at four o'clock, these "lazy" ones would often be waiting at his gate to go to their work. He was one day found dining with the priest, and the thing was so novel, that I expressed a pleasant surprise, when he answered: "I have consulted no one's opinion respecting the propriety of my doing so; I found," he added, "on coming here, this man a warm-hearted friend to the poor, doing all the good in his power, without any regard to party, and determined to treat him as a neighbour and friend, and have, as yet, seen no cause to regret it."

AUGHAGOWER

The Telegraph (8-3-1848).

The following are the names of persons who died from want in the parish of Aughagour, within the last fortnight: – March 1st: Duke Dawson:

interred without a coffin, on the fifth day after his death. Thomas Geraghty, of Garue, March 3rd: two sons of Francis Nugent, of Curdarngh, one 7 and the other 9 years old. February 28th: in Srakan, two children of Bryan Scahil. Also the grandfather and grandmother of the Scahils. At Letrun, Peter Gavan, who went into a roofless cabin, where he died. At Lanmore, Peter Mulholland, fell on the road from exhaustion, from which he was carried into a cabin – buried in 4 days after, without a coffin, in a turf bank. On Saturday last a poor woman carried her dead son in a rope, to the grave, but she was so exhausted she could not bury him. A charitable man opened a grave for the coffinless dead. March 6th: At Doon, the wife of Richard Freighan.

SWINFORD

Tyrawly Herald (13-4-1848).

On the 7th instant, the same Coroner held an inquest at Swinford, on the body of Sebina Conmee. Verdict, died from want and cold in the old waste forge, where she remained for two days. The Relieving Officer stated that she would not go into the Workhouse.

On the 8th instant the same Coroner held an inquest in the

parish of Bohola, on the body of Richard Cusack, who was found dead on the road side. Verdict, died from cold and hunger.

WESTPORT

Asenath Nicholson (1848).

A cabin was seen closed one day a little out of the town, when a man had the curiosity to open it, and in a dark corner he found a family of the father, mother and two children, lying in close compact. The father was considerably decomposed; the mother, it appeared, had died last, and probably fastened the door, which was always the custom when all hope was extinguished, to get into the darkest corner and die, where passers-by could not see them. Such family scenes were quite common, and the cabin was generally pulled down upon them for a grave. The man called, begging me to look in. I did not, and could not endure, as the famine progressed, such sights, as well as the first, they were too real, and these realities became a dread. In all my former walks over the island, by day or night, no shrinking or fear of danger ever retarded in the least my progress; but now, the horror of meeting living walking ghosts, or stumbling on the dead in my path at night, inclined me to keep within when necessity did not call.

GLENISLAND

The Telegraph (25-4-1848).

DEATHS FROM STARVATION IN GLENISLAND
On the 13th instant, widow Kelly and daughter, of Cloggan, coffined by Mr. John Carabine of Castlebar. On the 21st Anne Kelly, another daughter of the widows: and some days previous to the poor woman's decease a son of hers died also. The deaths of two more of her sons are hourly expected. On Sunday, Mary Faden, of Gravashbeg, and Pat McTigue, of Laplough. On the 2nd instant, Francis Lally. On the 10th, Pat Cormick, of Cloondaff. On the 17th, Nancy Cleary, of Bracklaugh. We have been furnished with a second list of persons in comparative affluence, drawing relief in Glanisland, while the really destitute are allowed to die of starvation.

ERREW

The Telegraph (14-3-1849).

DEATHS AT ERREW
Some days since a poor man named Kelly, with his wife and two children, from the parish of Mayo, called at the Monastery of Errew for some charity, which was given them. Next day, at a little distance from that excellent institution, the father and children were found dead. The bodies were put into coffins provided by the Christian Brethren at Errew, who had them buried. The poor woman was also supplied by them with other little requisites befitting her weak condition. To those who enjoy even a little of the good things of this life, we would say – take example by the Christian Brethren at Errew, who deny themselves for the comforting of God's afflicted.

NEPHIN

Tyrawly Herald (15-3-1849).

On Saturday last, Charles Atkinson, Esq., Coroner, held an inquest on the body of Martin Moffatt, at Nephin in the electoral division of Adragool. From the circumstances detailed before the jury, it appeared that himself and wife, and three children, had to live upon one stone of meal in the week, and that quantity was only sufficient to supply them with gruel for three days, so that for the remainder of the week they were without any description of food. The poor man's constitution was thus worn out and he died of exhaustion. A verdict to that effect was accordingly returned.

RATHNAMAUGH

Tyrawly Herald (13-12-1849).

On Saturday last, Peter Nolan, Esq., Coroner, held an inquest at Fortfreed, Rathnamaugh, on the body of a man, aged about 50 years. It appeared from evidence, that the deceased was a poor man wandering about one part of the country begging, whilst his wife and children frequented another. They all attended the Relief Depot together, and after getting their allowance divided it, the man retaining his own share and the wife and children theirs. Very little compassion was manifested towards him in the part of the country which he resorted, being sometimes obliged to sleep out in the ditches without the least covering. It also appeared that the portion of the relief which he received was 10 lbs., which he consumed in three days, remaining the rest of the week without any support unless the little that he got from some of his distant relatives. On the night of his death he was lying out at the end of a dwelling house, where he was heard moaning by the woman to whom it belonged. She sent out here maid with some new milk to him which he was unable to drink. The woman then alarmed her next neighbour, and the man was brought into the house where he died two hours afterwards. On the next morning they threw the body out on a dunghill, where they left it exposed, until they heard the Coroner was coming, when they again brought it in.

The jury found that the deceased came by his death in consequences of insufficiency of food and exposure to cold, both by day and night.

After the inquest the Coroner provided a coffin to have the body interred.

Response from Landlords

At the beginning of the Famine, in 1845, and continuing into 1846, many landlords reacted with compassion by reducing or deferring rent. Some provided funds to alleviate the starvation and continued to do so throughout the duration. The charity of others did not endure and, by 1948, many were enforcing wholesale eviction.

George, 3rd Marquis of Sligo, 1820 - 1896 (from "Westport House and the Brownes" by the Marquis of Sligo, 1981).

THE MARQUIS OF SLIGO

The Telegraph (22-7-1846).

THE MARQUIS OF SLIGO – It is with feelings of the most intense satisfaction that we lay before our readers, and the public in general, the welcome announcement made to us by the Rev. James Browne, P.P., of Ballintubber, who, on behalf of the Carranacun Relief Committee, addressed a letter to the Noble Marquis, stating the distress a portion of his tenantry was labouring under in that locality. This communication his lordship treated with the greatest courtesy and respect, manifesting, in a very high degree, those amiable traits of character which shed such a lustre over his departed sire. He instantly wrote back stating that he had given directions to Mr. Hildebrand to have the wants of his tenantry immediately attended to, which orders that excellent man is now carrying into effect in Mr. Browne's locality. This is a favour for which the Rev. gentleman expresses his deep debt of gratitude, and his parishioners their heartfelt thanks and manifold blessings. May his lordship live long to enjoy the comforts of his station, since he has so humanely and so timely come to the aid of those who "to beg were ashamed, and to work were not able." Oh! if appeals to the charity of our contiguous landlords will be of no avail, let at least this powerful example be not lost upon them.

SIR ROBERT BLOSSE LYNCH

The Telegraph (22-7-1846).

Sir Robert Blosse Lynch, Bart. – This high-minded young baronet has most promptly and most liberally come to the aid of the tenantry on his estates in Mayo. Those in the parish of Ballinrobe have been liberally attended to under the superintendence of Sir Robert's humane agent, Philip O'Reilly, Esq., who, with his family, has come to Mayo to carry out the humane instructions of his excellent employer.

THE EARL OF ARRAN

Mayo Constitution (23-7-1846).

Apprehensive of a scarcity of provisions among his tenantry, the Earl of Arran, through his active and kind agent, John Symes, Esq., has, with the most benevolent intention, purchased a large quantity of oatmeal which he is now distributing among those living on this part of his estate, upon the most liberal and easy terms. Mr. Walsh of Castlehill, and Mr. Jackson of Carramore, are likewise relieving distress on their properties, and taking benevolent steps in anticipation of apprehended want. Such conduct, we believe, is very general in this district, but more instances have not directly come under our observation. It is very laudable and will carry along with it its own reward – the pleasing consciousness of having done good, and a happy and prosperous tenantry as its results.

CHARLES O'MALLEY

The Telegraph (2-9-1846).

Benevolent Landlord – Charles O'Malley, Esq., of Lodge, Barrister-at-Law has, in the most humane manner supplied his tenantry with meal sufficient for their use until such time as they can grind their grain into meal. We hope his example may be imitated by others.

LORD LUCAN

Mayo Constitution (15-12-1846).

The inhabitants of Castlebar have come nobly forward to take advantage of the Earl of Lucan's proposition of subscribing £50 for each hundred collected by the inhabitants of this town. On Thursday last a meeting was convened by the Rev. Richard Gibbons, P.P., to whom the noble Earl's intentions were originally made known. The meeting was attended by a number of respectable inhabitants of the town. In taking the chair the reverend gentleman expressed a hope that their proceedings should be marked with a due regard to the feelings of all – that a Christian feeling should pervade that assembly, and each meeting which should assemble for the laudable purpose of relieving the poor. Union being strength, he called on all to unite to meet the common enemy – destitution and distress. He, therefore, hoped that the good feeling and unanimity which always distinguished the men of Castlebar, would not now be wanting.

LORD AVONMORE

The Telegraph (22-7-1846).

Lord Avonmore – This Nobleman has given directions to have immediate relief given to such of his tenantry as stand in need of aid in Ballintubber and elsewhere. This is as it should be.

BALLINA AND KILLALA

Tyrawly Herald (26-11-1846).

At this disastrous period when distress is so general, and provisions so exorbitantly high that they are placed beyond the reach of almost all the poor people, they, who would provide them and given them at cost price, without any profit, to the destitute, thereby relieving them from the necessity of purchasing at famine prices, must be considered as public benefactors. That we have some such benefactors in this neighbourhood will appear from the following fact: – Some short time since, Colonel Kirkwood, Walter J. Bourke, Esq., the Castle, Killala; John Knox, Esq., Castlerea; Major Gardiner, Farmhill; Oliver C. Jackson, Esq., Ballina, and Ernest Knox, Esq., Castlerea, privately subscribed the purchase money of a cargo of Indian meal. The meal was purchased for them at Liverpool by John Kirkwood, Esq., Killala, who acted in the transaction without any commission, and the meal was landed at Killala. It was brought from the quay, at Mr. Bourke's expense and lodged in his store, free of storage. He is now giving it out to the poor of Killala at first cost price, which must be a serious relief to the unfortunate people. Mr. Jackson, as one of the subscribers, obtained a portion of it, and had it brought to this town where he is having it sold, likewise, at first cost. He also sent a part of it to Swinford and Foxford where, upon its arrival, the famine price of meal fell to 19s.-6d. a hundred, thus affording indescribable relief to the poor, and rescuing them from the mercies of hard-hearted speculators. This is a bright example, and one which should be generally followed by the wealthier classes of society.

VISCOUNT DILLON

Tyrawly Herald (4-7-1847).

Upon the vast estate of Lord Dillon, and also upon that of Mr. Costello, Edmondstown, the sleepless and unrivalled exertions of Messrs. Strickland and Holmes have certainly been the means of good beyond estimation. Hundreds of lives must have been preserved by them, while the condition of thousand – had been preserved from the fearful pinchings of starvation. In fact, to detail the very effective exertions in the cause of the wretched would be to write more than convenience or space would warrant, but certainly not more than those gentlemen would deserve from the press in holding them forth to admiration, and in recommending them to be copied after as examples worthy the noblest to imitate.

SIR COMPTON DONVILLE

Mayo Constitution (15-2-1848).

AT a meeting of Sir Compton Donville's Tenants, living on the Townlands of Prison, Drimlonghra, Craggagh, Lisnolan, Castletoorly, and Loobnamuck, on his County of Mayo estate, held at Prison, on the 9th of February, 1848, Henry Waldron, J. P., Esq., in the chair.

The following resolutions were unanimously adopted:–

Proposed by James Hanabrow, and seconded by James Reilly.

Resolved – That the laudable efforts hitherto made by Sir Compton Donville, to improve his tenants, have justly earned for him the character of being the kindest of Landlords, and we declare that no language at our command can adequately convey how grateful we feel for the kind indulgence he has extended to us, during the last two years of appalling and unprecedented distress.

Proposed by Thomas Waldron, Esq.; seconded by Thomas Reilly.

Resolved - That were other Landlords actuated by the same benevolent feelings towards their tenants, the industry of the poor would be stimulated on finding that their labour, which forms their capital, was remunerated, and we would not have to deplore those agrarian outrages, and criminal excesses into which the unfortunate poor have been driven in other parts of Ireland.

Proposed by Bryan McHugh; seconded by Patt Shiel.

Resolved – That the humane and charitable wishes of our Landlord, have been always promptly seconded and cheerfully carried out by Thomas Sherrard, Esq., his intelligent and respected Agent, and we avail ourselves of the present opportunity to tender him our cordial thanks for his uniform kindness and attention.

George Henry Moore (1810 - 1870).

Proposed by Martin Barrett; seconded by Mark O'Donnell.

Resolved – That in justice to our good Landlord, and with a view of influencing others to imitate his example, we feel bound to proclaim that he has employed his tenants for the last two months, at great pecuniary sacrifice, in making permanent improvement on their own lands, and, to add to the obligations under which he has already placed us, he has given instructions to his respected Agent to erect a large and commodious Schoolhouse, for the purpose of diffusing the blessing of education among our children, and thus removing the many evils to which ignorance exposes them.

Signed on behalf of the tenants of Prison, Drimloughra, Craggagh, Lisnolan, Castleroorley and Loobnamuck.

HENRY WALDRON,
Chairman,

MARTIN BARRETT, *Secretary.*

GEORGE HENRY MOORE

*To the Editor of the FREEMAN,
Ballintubber, Ballyglass, Mayo,
June 21st, 1849.*

MY DEAR SIR - My attention having been directed by a friend, to a letter of mine published in the Freeman on the 2nd of this month, in which it appears that in the details of the frightful scenes of extermination which have been exhibited in these parishes for the last two years, to the destruction of a very large proportion of the people, I neglected, in the excitement of the moment, to do an act of justice to the humanity, benevolence, and feeling of one excellent landlord, Mr. Moore, of Moorehall, who owns a very large portion of Ballintubber. I now hasten to supply that omission, and in doing so, it affords me no little gratification to have this opportunity of expressing my own admiration of Mr. Moore's generosity and paternal kindness to his numerous tenantry, not only in these two parishes, but to the people on his other estates, in distant portions of the county. I have lived for many years in the midst of Mr. Moore's tenantry, and I never heard of a single tenant being evicted either by himself or his agent; of all his fine qualities there is none in which he so pre-eminently excels, nor for which he is so much admired, as his great tenderness for the poor, and, as an instance of how much he felt for the sufferings of the people, it is due to the grateful feelings of his tenantry to mention, that he sent over from London at an early stage of the famine a sum of £1,000 for the poor on his estates, as a free gift, besides orders to the steward to give a milch cow to every widow on his property. I beg to apologise for trespassing on your valuable space, and I have the honour to be, my dear Sir, yours most faithfully,

JAMES BROWN, P.P.,
of Ballintubber and Burriscarra.

CORANNA

George Moore netted £10,000 when his horse, Coranna, won the Chester Cup in 1846. He wrote to his mother at Moorehall: "No tenant of mine shall want for plenty of everything this year."

ANOTHER ATTACK – A carrier was a few days since stopped at the triangles, between Ballintubber and Westport, and robbed of his load of flour. The carman told the poor people that one of the flour barrels belonged to Mr. G. H. Moore's steward. The country people – to mark their gratitude to Mr. Moore, who has been unceasing in his acts of charity to those around him – put up the barrel on the cart, telling the carman they would die sooner than meddle with it.

(The Telegraph, 13-1-1847).

CHARITABLE GIFT – We have heard that Mrs. Maurice Blake, of Ballinafad, impressed with a sense of the misery of the small farmers in her locality, in addition to other contributions, has given the Rev. Mr. Browne, Carnacun, a splendid emerald ring, value £20, to be disposed of by lottery for benefit of the small farmers of that district. Mrs. Moore, Moorehall, has also placed several sums at the disposal of Mr. Browne, for a like object.

(Mayo Constitution, 14-8-1849).

Moore Hall, County Mayo.   *(Wynne Collection)*.

Relief Measures Fail Many

In an effort to restrict the numbers seeking admission to workhouses, a scheme known as Outdoor Relief was introduced, whereby food rations were distributed to the most destitute. Public works on roads, bridges, drainage, etc were also undertaken, offering employment so that people could earn money to buy food. Both measures provided much relief, but were often poorly and sometimes corruptly administrated.

PUBLIC WORKS AT NEWPORT

We were present on Monday last in the Court-house of Newport, where Sir R. A. O'Donel, Bart., Capt. Nugent, R. N., and the Rev. Peter Cannon, P.P., were assembled, using the most praiseworthy exertions to discover those persons who are in distress, in order to afford them employment. The plan they adopted to discriminate, and select those who were most in want, was such as to attain their end. Lists were made out of the heads of families in each district and the number depending upon them for support. It appeared to us that the sole object these gentlemen had in view was to extend relief, where most required, without partiality, favour or affection. They issued tickets, directed to the Inspectors and Overseers of the Public Works carrying on under the Board of Works, directing them to employ within the parish of Newport five-hundred destitute persons, who are now actively engaged earning 10d. per day, to be paid weekly, in cash.

The Telegraph (24-6-1846).

NO WAGES

Numerous, and we regret to state, well founded complaints, have been made to us from Turlough, Islandeady, Castlebar, Ballinrobe, Newport, Westport, Aughagower and Ballyhean, as to the manner in which Public Works are being carried out – but particularly the way in which the poor wretches employed on them are paid their wages. Many of those creatures, pale and haggard, have declared to us that for two, three, four and five weeks! they have not been paid their wages: that when they apply for it in the morning they are told "to call in the evening": in the evening they are desired "to call in the morning": that they are harassed travelling some six or seven miles, looking for this money.

The Telegraph (12-8-1846).

SHIPMENTS OF MEAL

GOVERNMENT MEAL – The following is, we believe, an accurate return of the quantity of meal received, and dates of issue to the several localities in the Westport Coast Guard station, and placed under the control of that efficient and humane officer, Capt. Nugent R. N.:–

Clifden station, June 16th ... ...30 Tons.
Belmullet ditto, June 17th ... ...20 ditto.
Achilbeg, Clare Island, Boffin,
  and Innisturk, June 17th ... ...20 ditto.
Clifden station, June 19th ... ...20 ditto.
Achil station, June 20th ... ...20 ditto.
Bullsmouth & Achilbeg station, June 22d ... ...20 ditto.
Newport and Rostrunk station, June 22d ... ...20 ditto.

Her Majesty's Steamer Rhadamanthus, arrived at Clifden on the 21st ultimo with a cargo of meal. Her Majesty's Steamer Dee, arrived at Innislyre on the 22n ultimo with a cargo of meal for the depot of Westport, under charge of Captain Perceval. The activity and zeal of Sir James Dombrain, Inspector-General of Coast Guards, is most unremitting in the allocation of the supplies, in which he is assiduously assisted by Captain Nugent and the respective Commanders and Chief Officers of that force.

The Telegraph (1-7-1846).

FAVOURITISM

Others complained that they had tickets for work but would not be allowed into any work, the overseers having their own favourites: we have seen some of those tickets dated so far back as the first and second weeks in July last – signed, "George Ormsby, A. Bole and James Malley." Those tickets have been set at nought by gombeen overseers, while others, who stand in no need of work, are employed on tickets obtained by "misrepresentation." We can name "overseers" who have discharged the widow's son, her only support, and taken in at the same time, members of families who have tons of meal sold on time at 25s per cwt. Is not this gross fraud? Is it not in direct violation of the order from the Board of Works, and contrary to every law human and Divine? It is an insult to the individuals who issue tickets, and an injury to the poor widows and orphans deprived of bread by factious overseers – who for a glass or two of poteen whiskey turn them off to make room for favourites, that stand in no need of such work.

The Telegraph (12-8-1846).

OFFICE OF PUBLIC WORKS, CUSTOM-HOUSE, DUBLIN.

ADVERTISEMENT.

To Carpenters, Workers in Hard Wood, Smiths, &c.,
IN THE COUNTY OF MAYO.

THE COMMISSIONERS OF PUBLIC WORKS will be prepared to receive Tenders addressed to this Office, on or before the 30th instant, from Workers in Hard Wood, manufacturing Smiths, &c., for delivering to their Agents at the undermentioned Stations, the Implements in Wood and Iron hereinafter enumerated, patterns, plans, and specifications for the making of which, may be seen at this Office, and at the Offices of the Engineers in the several districts throughout the county where Public Works are being carried on.

The Commissioners do not pledge themselves to accept the lowest, or any offer, unless the terms proposed are fair and reasonable. They hold a large stock of every class of Working Implements in their Stores in Dublin, with which they will be prepared to supply the remote Works, should unreasonable demands from local artificers, or delay in the supply, compel them to do so; and thus the advantage of the employment which the manufacture of the Implements would afford, will be lost to the neighbourhood.

Parties tendering are to state the number of each respective class of Implements they will be able to deliver, and the time they will require to make their deliveries.

Tenders to be addressed to JOS. C. WALKER, Esq,, Secretary, and endorsed --"Tenders for Implements."

(By Order,)
JOS. C. WALKER,
Secretary.

Dated this 16th day of October, 1846.

PROVINCE OF CONNAUGHT—COUNTY OF MAYO.

DEPOTS.	Wheel Barrows.	Hand Barrows.	Clay Picks.	Quarry Picks.	Falling Bars, pointed at each end.
Ballaghaderreen	500	10	250	25	50
Ballina	500	10	250	25	50
Ballinrobe	500	10	250	25	50
Belmullet	500	10	250	25	50
Castlebar	1000	20	500	50	100
Foxford	500	10	250	25	50
Hollymount	500	10	250	25	50
Newport	500	10	250	25	50
Westport	750	15	375	37	75

SUSPENSION OF PUBLIC WORKS

The drainage of the river of Castlebar is to be discontinued on the 15th of August. We must lament this order as it will be the ruin of many hundred poor persons, who daily subsisted by looking over the battlements of our bridges, watching the government humbugs, up to their knees in marsh and mud, taking levels, not perhaps of the river, but of the emaciated faces by which those whisker-andoes are surrounded. Pshaw! we shall not longer submit to be treated thus: if the country is to be taxed for the relief of distress let the distressed be employed. Our river has not yet been meddled with, notwithstanding our town is filled with government hangers-on, sent over to lull poor Pat to rest – in fact, to fill his empty stomach with hopes of regailing it soon by the fruits of his labour - an expectation into which many have been led by seeing those strangers going from plot to plot along the river with their maps and pencils, as though planning out that work which is to cease on the 15th of August. How many persons are employed on the Clydagh and Turlough Drainage? Will the officers of the Board state why the people are kept idle while the weather is so favourable for such work?

The Telegraph (16-6-1847).

TUBBERCURRY

We here first encountered the public works so called. These consisted in making new roads and altering old ones, in many cases worse than useless, and obviously undertaken without judgment, for the mere sake of employment. Independently of the moral effects of useless labour – which it is impossible should be otherwise than listlessly pursued – it was melancholy and degrading in the extreme to see the women and girls withdrawn from all that was decent and proper, and labouring in mixed gangs on public roads. Not only in digging with the spade, and with the pick, but in carrying loads of earth and turves on their backs, and wheeling barrows like men, and breaking stones, are they employed. My heart often sunk within me at the obviously deteriorating effects of such occupation, while the poor neglected children were crouched in groups around the bits of lighted turves in the various sheltered corners along the line.

The pay was 6d. and 7d. per day to the girls and women, and 8d. to the men; which being the lowest we met with anywhere, though never exceeding 10d.

W. J. Bennett (6-3-1847).

EMPLOYMENT AT BALLYHEANE

EFFECTS OF EMPLOYMENT – We had much gratification, the other day, in observing the improvement and comforts

Women were employed on relief works for as little as 6 old pence a day.

which result from employment in lieu of the present outdoor relief. We allude to the tenantry on a small estate, the property of John Finn, Esq., in the neighbourhood of Ballyhean. A grant for drainage was obtained by J. C. Larminie, Esq., Mr. Finn's agent, by which there are several members of families employed at wages varying from 10d. to 1s. per day. By this means upwards of ninety

families are removed from the relief lists of that parish, and the people are remuneratively employed, with benefits to themselves and immediate and lasting advantage to the landlord. We regret that others have not followed the example of Mr. Larminie, which would tend to the good of all, landlord and tenant; more especially in the season of existencies, as persons so employed would not be at the mercy of government officials – to be fed or starved at will.

Mayo Constitution (3-8-1847).

BOARD OF WORKS

Daily Average Number of Persons Employed on the Roads during the Week ending the 7th November, 1847.

Counties and Baronies.	Arti-ficers.	Labourers.		Women.	Boys.
		Able-bodied.	Infirm.		
MAYO.					
1. Burrishoole . .	..	688	4	29	8
2. Carra	..	1,554	15	86	69
3. Clanmorris . .	..	1,284	4	69	24
4. Costello . . .	..	1,097	4	66	47
5. Erris	..	811	..	4	..
6. Gallen. . . .	..	887	8	72	57
7. Kilmaine . . .	..	2,441	7	34	186
8. Murrisk . . .	..	722	..	26	17
9. Tirawley . . .	..	1,080	35	44	40
Total in Mayo .	..	10,564	77	430	448

Parliamentary Papers 1847

BELMULLET

MR. R. HAMILTON, Temporary Inspector at Belmullet, to the POOR LAW COMMISSIONERS: – November 13, 1847.

During the past week, I have visited every portion of my district except the extreme western part of Belmullet electoral division; and I regret to state, that distress, – indeed, judging by the appearance of the people, I may say starvation, – appears nearly general throughout it, but more particularly in the electoral division of Binghamstown, where the poor really are in a sad state, their only food bad turnips, and their supply of them limited; many have nothing to subsist on but the roots of weeds. The relieving officer has several hundreds on his books; but the poor people are afraid to venture a second time to Ballina, the distance being nearly 40 miles. The British Association having placed a small quantity of provisions at my disposal, I have given out some of it in this district through the medium of the clergymen, in order to prevent death from starvation, but have confined the relief principally to destitute females and children under a certain age. There are seven established schools in this electoral division; and I hope to have 1,000 children on Monday next receiving their daily rations in these establishments. There is no proprietor or person of any respectability who takes the least interest in the welfare of the unfortunate poor in this district.

Although Belmullet division is much distressed, still I do not think it can be as bad as Binghamstown, because I hardly went through a village in it I did not see a dog in every house, and I am quite certain when they can keep a dog they cannot be starving. The feeding of the children at established schools will likewise succeed in this division, and I shall have rations issued at several on Monday.

I shall report, from time to time, on the state of this district, which I have no doubt will require other sources before long beside the rates.

Parliamentary Papers (1847).

OUTDOOR RELIEF CASTLEBAR

At a meeting of the Vice-Guardians, held at the Workhouse, Castlebar, on Saturday, the 18th instant, the following numbers, in addition to those already enroled, were put on the outdoor relief lists of the several electoral divisions:–

		Discharged from Workhouse to out-door relief.
Addergoole	204	3
Islandeady	78	0
Balla	53	0
Drum	46	12
Castlebar	301	35
Breaffy	72	0
Ballyheane	187	0
Ballintubber	163	4
Straide & Turlough	218	6
	1,322	60

Total 1,382

This a very large number for one day, and yet there are as many shouting for relief as ever. We have before stated our conviction that imposition, on the part of applicants, will be practised on the managers of the relief unless they appoint a medical man to give certificates, as many will say their families are in fever, when such is not the case. We hope the Guardians, to protect the rate payers from imposition, will immediately appoint a medical officer, to certify in such cases. The salary given to a medical gentleman will be a mere trifle, when we consider the saving that may be effected thereby to the Union at large. This plan, we find is adopted in other Irish Unions, and we believe, with good effect.

The Telegraph (22-12-1847).

SHORT MEASURE

DR. DEMPSTER to the COMMISSIONERS:– January 4, 1848.

Referring to a former report, wherein I stated my suspicions that the meal contractors, engaged by the Vice-Guardians to supply the outdoor rations to the poor people of these districts, were not honestly fulfilling their duties, I have the honour to annex, for the information of the Poor Law Commissioners, a report received last evening from one of the sub-relieving officers, Myles Nally, for Robeen electoral division, corroborating my suspicions; and I feel satisfied a like practice is being carried on in the other electoral divisions.

On my way to Claremorris, on the 28th ultimo, I called on Nally, and gave him instructions to weigh the meal delivered to some of the unfortunate creatures, and to let me know the result.

I think the contractor could be indicted for fraud; and I respectfully request the case may be laid before the law officers, as I should like to make an example of such persons, who rob the poor of their allowance and defraud the Union.

ENCLOSURE

I, MYLES NALLY, assistant relieving officer for the electoral division of Robeen, do hereby certify that I weighed the meal of the following persons on Sunday, the 2nd instant, and found them to be short as follows:–

	lbs.	oz.
No. 3 on Relief list, Mary Giles, Carranore short	3	8
No. 52, entitled to 24.5 lbs., Peter Grady, do. do	2	13
No. 61 and 62, Mary Boyle and Pat Stanton, Shirelough, do	1	12
No. 96, Richard Gaven, Girlough, do.	2	0
No. 73, 24.5 lbs., Biddy Little, Brackford, do	2	0
No. 68, 14 lbs., Mary Mohan, do. do.	2	0
No. 86, Mary Kerns, Carrabrine, do.	1	0
No. 74, 10.5 lbs., Mary Kerns, Cloonchina, do.	1	0
No. 85, 14 lbs., Thady Golam, Cloonagh, do.	1	4

The above to be short can be proved by me and them. Given under my hand this 3rd day of January, 1948,

MYLES NALLY, A.R.O., Robeen.

Many others were also short.

M. N.

Parliamentary Papers (1847).

CHILD (12), SUPPORTS FAMILY

To the Editor of the Telegraph:
SIR – I hope that you will take it into one of your columns a melancholy and most grievous affair which occurred in the townland of Mucknaugh, in the Parish of Islandeady, and barony of Carra, and county of Mayo. A few of the destitute of said townland, which is the property of Sir Roger Palmer, were supplied with relief tickets to work on a line of road about four miles from their home, which was very harsh on them to walk twice a day going to work and returning home; and in consequence of want and distress they were very happy to enjoy it; but the want of subsistence and the severity of the weather soon beat up some of those persons, amongst whom were John O'Gowan and Michael Heraghty, who were confined to their beds, and in a few days after John M'Gowan departed this life through want and starvation, he having no means to support himself and family but whatever he earned on the road. He was a man about forty years of age, able bodied, but want of subsistence caused his death; and his corpse remained three days and three nights unburied until Mr.

Rowland provided all necessaries for his interment. He died on Wednesday, the 16th of December and was buried on Saturday, the 19th.

Poor Heraghty is not expected to recover. He has six in family and no means of supporting them but the earning of one individual, a child about twelve years old, who works on the road; and there are many others in the same locality nearly in a state of starvation, who have long families, from six to ten in each house, and only one relief card for the householder, and all the rest as well able to use grub as him, – so it is hoped that every locality will get its conveniency, and that it should be made known to the County Surveyor, who is a knowledgeable man. If the districts were made known to him, he is willing and at readiness at all times to appoint every man at his own conveniency.

Your most humble and obedient servant,

JOHN M'LAUGHLIN,
December 20th, 1846.

The Telegraph (30-12-1848).

INQUESTS

On the same day, he held an inquest, at Kilcummin, on the body of James Drisdale, a labourer on the Public Works.

On Saturday evening he was proceeding to where the Pay Clerk was, an on his way he fell exhausted on the road. On the following morning he was found dead on the spot where he fell and after the examination of Dr. Neilson, a verdict of "death from starvation" was returned.

On Monday, the same coroner held an inquest, at Saltfield, in the Parish of Kilgarvin, on the body of Patt Howley. The deceased was employed on the Public Works, and on his way home on Saturday evening he fell to the ground through weakness. In this condition he was found by a man who was passing by, and on being asked what was the matter, the only words he could articulate were "hunger and weakness." After the examination of Dr. Whittaker, a verdict of "death from starvation" was returned.

Tyrawly Herald (11-2-1847).

RELIEVING OFFICERS CHARGED

The inquest ·was held before Richard O'Grady, Esq., coroner, on the body of Patrick Gallagher, of Templemore:

Bryan Dunleavy stated that deceased slept in his brother's house the night before he died, and was speaking to him; deceased told him that he was not getting the relief because he would not go to break stones, and he was too weak to do so; he was begging about the neighbourhood; appeared to be in a weak state, but did not complain of illness; his clothes were very bad: after he left his brother's house, saw him dead outside a door in the village.

Martin–, who was formerly relieving officer for the electoral division of Straid, having resigned in favour of his brother, stated that he knew the deceased, who was on his relief list, and gave him relief regularly until the 25th of March last; he had no house or land; he was healthy and able-bodied up to that time and, as such, was disentitled to out-door relief, and the Castlebar guardians took his name off the list; he refused in-door relief, and afterwards applied for out-door relief, but witness stated he could give him nothing but in-door relief, which he again refused; there were few who were more destitute, or fitter objects for relief.

Our correspondent who favoured us with the above, writes that the police were so satisfied of the culpability of the relieving officers, that they charged them as accessories to the poor man's death in their requisition to the coroner.

Mayo Constitution (16-5-1848).

DIED WAITING FOR PAY CLERK

On the same day he held an inquest at Coolcran on the body of Patrick Redington. The deceased was employed at the public works, and on Saturday morning he went to the hill of Gurteens to meet the pay clerk where, in company of other labourers he remained until night, but no clerk making his appearance, the others went off and he remained behind. Having got quite weak, he requested a girl who was passing to tell his wife to come and meet him, and upon the wife's arriving at the place she found him dead. After the examination of Dr. Whittaker, a verdict of "death from starvation" was returned.

Tyrawly Herald (25-2-1847).

FRAUDULENT WEIGHTS AND MEASURES

An instance of the importance of the proper and energetic discharge of the duties of the office of Inspector of Weights and Measures, occurred at Westport Quarter Sessions on Tuesday last, on the trial of an appeal for a conviction for £5, against a man named Martin Walsh. It appeared that he was employed in Westport distributing outdoor relief, and in the establishment where this fellow doled out the curtailed allowance to the poor, two false weights and a false beam, which was so constructed that it would require three pounds weight to turn the scale in favour of the poor man, were seized. The Court very properly affirmed the conviction, with costs, and concurred with the Magistrates in supporting Mr. Sheridan in the discharge of his important duties, denouncing the conduct of the appellant as the grossest case of injustice he had ever heard of, and stating it as his opinion that the parties should be punished criminally for such gross conduct.

This is not the first instance of those fellows who are entrusted with the disbursement of relief being detected by Mr. Sheridan in such acts of misconduct; and we trust it will be a warning to others whose conduct has been rather suspicious.

Mayo Constitution (25-4-1848).

DISMISSED FOR IDLENESS

The following is the Labour Return for the last week:–

Electoral Divisions	No. in Gangs	Total Days' Work	No. Boxes of Stone Broken	No. of Labourers Struck off.	Observations
Addergoole	114	605$1/2$	445$1/2$	2	
Balla	68	340	272	2	
Ballintubber	117	437	211	2	
Ballyhean	150	365	101	17	Overseer cautioned and labourers, that if a larger task was not performed in future, names should be struck out, rations stopped, and overseer dismissed.
Breaffy	67	288$1/4$	146	2	Ditto ditto ditto
Castlebar	77	318$1/2$	-	-	Employed in workhouse grounds, quarry having been refused by owner.
Drum	150	761$1/2$	1,005$1/4$	54	Overseer dismissed.
Islandeady	65	256	204$1/2$	8	
Strade	123	489	632	18	
Turlough	57	227	212	35	
	988	4,087$3/4$	3,289$1/4$	140	

This return only shows the quantity of stone broken; portions of the men were employed in quarrying the stone and preparing it for the breakers. The weather was very unfavourable.

On the examination of the books, 140 labourers were struck off for idleness or absence from the work, by which they and their families, from 700 to 800 individuals, lost their rations.

Parliamentary Papers (2-2-1848).

TOO ABLE BODIED

TO THE HONOURABLE FREDERICK CAVENDISH.

Sir – On Sunday last, while walking up Gallowshill, in this town, my feelings were appealed to on behalf of a poor family (four in number) actually dying of starvation within a few acres of the so-called Workhouse. To ascertain the truth of what I heard I entered the miserable hut, and on the cold earth, on a handful of old straw, I found two children lying, the mother also sick, but struggling to sit up, watching by her children. Finding hunger was the cause of their ailment, I supplied them with the price of food for that day and the next. The poor father, with tears in his eyes, declared to me they had not tasted of food since the previous Friday morning, save one half-penny worth of raw turnips: that, as a last resort, he must have recourse to which one of his family never was guilty of – namely, ROBBERY!

I asked him why he had not been relieved by the Vice Guardians? He said – "He knew not: he attended the meetings of the Board of the two previous Thursdays, and on the latter day was ordered off, being an able-bodied man." Heavens, such an able bodied man! Why, the father, wife, and two children, would not, I am positively sure, weigh ten stone!

JOHN HOGAN,
Castlebar (February 5th, 1849).

The Telegraph (7-2-1849).

HELD LAND – NO RELIEF

CASTLEBAR – On Monday last a poor man named John O'Hara, a native of Cappagh, about a mile from Castlebar, called at the shop of Mr. Brennan, in this town, to get from him a writing to the relieving officer for some food,

as he was dying of starvation. He got the note, and on it obtained relief, shortly after which the poor man died on the road near the workhouse, on his way home. It appears that about a fortnight before he obtained provisional relief, but did not pass the board, the driver of Sir S. O'Malley certifying he held land. The poor victim of the Gregory Clause tumbled his house, and sold the timber to buy food, but failed in giving the land up to Sir Samuel, as he could not obtain access to the worthy Baronet or any person authorised by him to receive possession. For eight days

previous to his death no sort of food entered his mouth save a little turnip juice obtained from his neighbours. At last he sunk in death as above stated. Mr. Kelly, one of the Vice Guardians, who was waited on by Mr. Brennan, gave an order for a coffin on the "undertaker," as also an order for the immediate admission to the workhouse, of deceased's brother, who likewise exhibited convincing proofs of fast approaching dissolution from the same cause. The deceased has left two children as a legacy to the union.

The Telegraph (7-3-1849).

TURNED AWAY

STARVATION AND DEATH – On Wednesday last a poor man from Turlough, applied at the Workhouse of this town for in or out-door relief, which was denied him, for what cause we have not learned. The poor fellow in a few hours after was found dead on the road between Castlebar and Turlough, having sunk from exhaustion.

The Telegraph (14-3-1849).

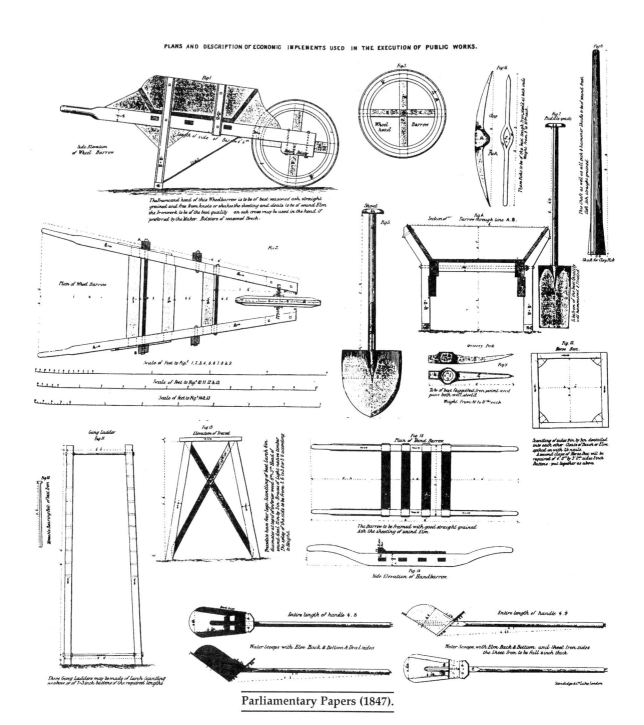

PLANS AND DESCRIPTION OF ECONOMIC IMPLEMENTS USED IN THE EXECUTION OF PUBLIC WORKS.

Parliamentary Papers (1847).

Charity

Many groups at home and abroad were involved in charitable works. Clergy of all denominations were prominent in relief measures. The Society of Friends (Quakers) saved many lives by providing soup kitchens in several areas. There were also some individual efforts and some who worked among the sick fell victim of fever themselves.

AID FOR CASTLEBAR

To reain silent while hunger and death surrounds our dwellings would be an act of unpardonable criminality, and one for which we could offer no palliation. Within the last week the cry of famine in this town has alarmingly increased, so much so that we are actually horrified at the prospect before us. This vast increase of pauperisation has been occasioned by the multitudes struck off the public works, who have no means whatever now left to them to obtain subsistence. While on the works many of them were enabled to pay for soup and give a trifle for the cheap meal supplied by the Evangelical Relief Committee in this town, as well as by the Rev. Mr. Stoney, who supplies a great number with stirabout almost daily at his residence.

On Friday last the number of individuals supplied with cheap meal, and also gratuitously, by the Evangelical Committee, was over six-hundred. Yet, the demand could not be kept pace with. The haggard appearance of the poor applicants was soul-harrowing to look on, while their lamentations at being struck off the works is far beyond our power of description.

On Saturday last the Treasurer, Rev. Mr. Jordan, was honoured with another draft for £25 from the Rev. Mr. James, Secretary to the Irish Evangelical or Independent Relief Committee of London. This makes £100 received from that benevolent body for the relief of the poor in and about this town. This cry for gratuitous relief is now become irresible, unless the people are allowed to lie down and die! Horrible alternative, while the granaries of the kingdom are creaking beneath the weight of food! But what of this when the poor have no money to buy! From the farmers they can get no work, for they have discharged their farm servants, who are now become applicants for English charity at the relief depots in Castlebar.

The Telegraph (31-3-1846).

A GLENISLAND NEIGHBOUR

A PEASANT SAMARITAN – Laurence McHugh, of the village of Barnastang, Glenisland, with a family of six children, himself and wife, in all eight persons, were on Monday morning last in that low degree, from hunger that, as our informant states, the most of them could not survive until night. With much difficulty the poor man made his way to the house of Patt Malley, a neighbour, who is in great want himself, having no provisions but as he buys the market: still the Irish heart beat in his bosom: "he could not," he said, "see his neighbours die while God left him anything" and he forthwith went out, took one of his four sheep, and handed it over to poor McHugh, to kill for himself and family. Reader, go then and do likewise. We know the landlord, Sir Roger Palmer, Bart., is not aware of the wants of his tenantry: if he were so we are confident that immediate relief would be ordered by him for their use. Malley! may his Herd, like the widow's cruise of oil, never diminish.

The Telegraph (7-10-1846).

Children begging from a gentleman traveller.

TURLOUGH

ACKNOWLEDGMENT – The Rev. Paul MacGreal, P.P., of Turlough, gratefully acknowledges a remittance of £15 in aid of the relief of the poor of his parish, from the India Poor Relief Fund, through their Secretary, T. L. Synnot, Esq.

The Telegraph (7-10-1846).

BALLYHAUNIS RELIEF COMMITTEE

At a meeting of the Ballyhaunis Relief Committee, held on Friday, the 4th of December, instant, Edward P. MacDonnell, Esq., in the Chair, the following resolutions were unanimously adopted:–

Proposed by the Rev. Eugene Coyne, P.P.; seconded by Dr. Davis:

Resolved – That the former Relief Committee be dissolved, and that the Rev. John Finn, O.S.A., be appointed Treasurer to the Committee.

Proposed by Rev. P. Duffy, P.P.; seconded by Austin Crean, Esq.:

Resolved – That our best thanks being due, are cheerfully given to our late Treasurer,

Charles Strickland, Esq., for his invaluable services during the past trying season; and also for his having most liberally taken upon himself the whole expense attending the sale of Meal at reduced prices, and having returned the several Loans without any deduction whatever.

Proposed by Rev. Richard Prendergast; seconded by Ignatius O'Donel, Esq.:

Resolved – That these Resolutions be published in the Mayo Telegraph.

EDWARD P. MacDONNELL, Chairman.

The Telegraph (9-12-1846).

IRISH RELIEF ASSOCIATION

We have seen with pleasure the rapid progress of this charitable association, in their laudable efforts to raise subscriptions to help to feed their starving fellow-country-men. Each day their efforts are crowned with success, the effects of which we trust are nigh at hand to us. We have been informed that a sum of £20 has been forwarded to W. Campbell,

Esq., for the poor of Ballycroy, with a promise of further donations, to be expended by him in selling meal at reduced prices. We have also heard that £500 worth of meal has been granted to the Rev. Mr. Pounden, Rector of Westport, for the relief of the poor of that district; and also a supply promised to the Rev. Edward Nangle, for the Achill poor.

We sincerely trust that the association will be liberally contributed to by those able to spare of their abundance as from the character of the gentlemen conducting the fullest reliance, can be placed in the fair distribution," if the funds committed to their trust.

Mayo Constitution (15-12-1846).

THE POOR OF BALLINA

The Rev. Francis Kinkead has applied the munificent donation of A. K. L. for the special relief of the poor of Ballina, in the following manner:–

Twenty pounds have been laid out in redeeming from the Pawn-office, one article of day or night covering for each recipient of this bounty – one-hundred-and-thirty persons have had in this manner some useful article of dress to protect them from the inclemency of the Winter, restored to them. It was painful to see the hundreds who had to go away disappointed, and the proof of the greatness and prevalence of distress, the multitude of tickets in the possession of each person demonstrated. The Pawnbroker's generously aided the design of the noble donor by dispensing with the interest due on the several deposits which were released.

Mr. Kinkead has allocated the remaining ten pounds for the purchase of flannel, to make warm inner clothing for such sick persons as shall be recommended by the local

Distributing clothing to the poor.

medical gentlemen; and the ladies of the benevolent society have most kindly undertaken the task of purchasing the material and making the articles for the claimants.

Tyrawly Herald (31-12-1846).

A NATIONAL SCHOOL IN CHESHIRE

In the darkness of this day of affliction, it is comforting to see the sympathy evinced for the poor by the kind people of England, even the "children taking part in the good work, and exhibiting a noble self denial that they may give to those who need. The following letter addressed to the Rev. Richard St. George, Rector of Crossmolina, needs no comment to impress its worth:

Rev. Sir – We, the children belonging to the Moulton National School, in the Parish of Davenharm (Cheshire), having heard from our beloved patroness, Mrs. Harper, of the distress that is so prevalent in our sister island, have given up our annual treat to the relief of our suffering sisters in Ireland; trusting that God, of His abundant mercy, will soon turn the "scarcity and dearth which they now suffer into plenty and cheapness." We humbly trust that our offering (small as it may appear), will be accepted by those who have kindly undertaken to alleviate the sufferings of our brethren. As we have bountifully received of the Lord, so we also freely give. We here insert our names – M. Whitlow, L. Garner, E. Dickinson, E. Darlington, W. Buckley, L. Bateman, G. Dickinson, J. Downes, R. Ravenscroft, W. Williams, Jos Astbury, E. Whitton, M. Astbury, James Presten, W. Hicken, L. Kemmerley, T. Hutchinson, and of thirty other children.

Tyrawly Herald (31-12-1846).

BALLINA AND ARDNAREE RELIEF COMMITTEE

At a meeting of the Ballina and Ardnaree Relief Committee, held in the Court-house on Tuesday, the 19th of January, the Managers of the Soup Kitchen handed in a statement of their proceedings for the last week with the accounts.

It appeared that they distributed each day 1,387 quarts of soup to 563 families at the expense of £23-12s.-1d. The accounts and vouchers were examined and found correct.

It was resolved, that the thanks of the meeting be given to them for the zeal and attention they manifested in the arduous duty.

Resolved – That Dr. Smith and Messrs. J. M'Hugh, and James Higgins, be appointed managers of the Soup Kitchen for the ensuing week.

Resolved – That to enable the Committee to maintain the Soup Kitchen large and continued support is indispensably requisite.

Resolved – That while we again return our heartfelt thanks to those who have so generously aided us in our exertions to relieve our famishing fellow creatures, we implore them to continue their support, to enable us, not only to continue the daily distribution of soup to those now receiving it, but to extend it to some of those who have not hitherto obtained any, though eagerly seeking it.

Subscriptions, as heretofore, will be thankfully received by the Rev. Joseph Verschoyle, Ballina, Rector of the Parish, by the Secretaries, by the Provincial and National Banks, or by any member of the Committee.

Resolved – That in consequence of the indisposition of the Rev. F. Kinkead, Henry Crofton, Esq., be appointed Secretary, with authority to sign cheques jointly with the Rev. Mr. Conway.

– J. VERSCHOYLE, Chairman.

Tyrawly Herald (21-1-1847).

FREIZE AND BROGUES

For Naked Labourers on the Island of Achill

The Christian public are informed that numbers of poor creatures attend the Achill Dispensary, unable to continue on the public works for want of clothing. For six or seven months they have not been able to purchase a single article – are now disposing of their pigs, poultry, sheep and lambs, even blankets have been sold to procure food; yet carts with provisions pass through the Island, not only unmolested, but have been assisted by the Islanders. This forms no small claim for relief on those who value the peace of the country.

A freize frock coat, costing seven or eight shillings, or a pair of brogues, costing five or six shillings, would enable a poor man to support himself and family for the Winter.

Webs of freize, or brogues, sent to Mr. Willis, 36 Bride-street, Dublin. Orders on the Postmaster, Newport, Mayo, in my favour, by which country freize, or brogues, can be purchased, will be thankfully received, carefully expended and accounted for in a report to each subscriber.

One-hundred-and-thirty-nine frock coats and waist-coats, nineteen monkey jackets, and one-hundred-and-sixty-five pair of brogues have already been distributed.

NEASON ADAMS, M.D.,
Honorary Physician to the
Achill Dispensary.

Achill Missionary Herald (January-1846).

KINCON

The Dean of Killala has much pleasure in stating, that he has been so far assisted by some benevolent individuals, as to enable him to make two free distributions of oatmeal, according to a most strictly scrutinised list, of the most destitute in and around the village of Kincun, to a distance of two miles, and in quantities of one stone, or half stone, to each family according to its numerical account, and other circumstances. On the 18th instant this extended to 62 families: on the 14th, 68. He hopes to continue this weekly.

Tyrawly Herald (21-1-1847).

ROSSPORT SOUP-KITCHEN

W. J. Bennett (18-3-1847).

Among other persons who had left his vocation and emigrated was the schoolmaster, so that the school was now abandoned. From the assistance granted by Wm. Forster, on behalf of the Society of Friends, the school-house was fitted up into a soup-kitchen. We attended the giving out of the soup; and it appeared under the excellent management of the lady before mentioned, and S. Bourn's son. Without this timely

assistance, he declared, a large portion of his tenantry must have perished. The poor people came a very long way, from other districts, in hopes of partaking of the bounty, and were not sent empty away.

DEATH OF THE REV. P. POUNDEN

Approving as we highly do of the following comments from the Dublin Evening Mail, we transfer them into our columns:

"With unaffected sorrow – a sorrow in which the public, to a very large extent, will share – we have to announce the demise of the Rev. Patrick Pounden, Rector of Westport. This excellent and devoted servant of God died, on Saturday last, of fever, caught in the discharge of his sacred duties, and rendered fatal by the exhaustion of mind and body in the course of his unremitting labours for the relief of the poor and needy – the famishing and the dying – in his extensive district. Indeed, he may be said to have mortgaged his life for the benefit of his fellow-creatures: for having guaranteed to the relief funds of his

neighbourhood no less a supply than seventy pounds a week, to be raised partly out of his own means, and partly by the subscription of the benevolent – it is little to be wondered at that the requisite exertion, united to the discharge of his ministerial functions, visiting from house to house, giving food to the hungry, and spiritual advice to the sick and dying, should have proved too much for his strength, and that he fell a victim to the calamity which afflicts the country.

"Mr. Pounden was a man distinguished through life for the accomplishments of a scholar and the virtues of a Christian. He was well known and beloved in the religious world; and was highly esteemed, not only as an able advocate of the Established Church, but as a prodtable example of what a Christian pastor should be. By a dispensation of Providence which, however, mysterious to us, was doubtless to himself acceptable and welcome, he has been taken away from the scene of his early labours. His end appears to have been what he would have chosen for himself – death in the service of God, and in the cause of his fellow-creatures."

The Telegraph (7-4-1847).

CASTLEBAR COFFIN FUND

Sir – I will feel much obliged by your publishing the accompanying letter from Mr. John Gibbons, of Westport. The thanks and gratitude of the people of this town and neighbourhood are justly due to the benevolent gentlemen, for his generous contribution to our coffin fund. You are, I believe, already aware that the Rev. Mr. Atkins, Mr. Patrick Walsh, and I were requested to solicit the subscriptions of the people of the town for the purpose, if possible, of sustaining this fund

Clergy of all denominations were prominent in relieving distress.

and enabling us to continue the humane work of burying, WITH COFFINS, the numerous dead. I respectfully suggest that this should be our last resort. The towns-people are actually harassed with such applications, and in this instance they should be left to themselves. They are now aware that such a fund is being raised, and any person, whose charity prompts him, can of of own accord send his contribution to Mr. William Larminie, the treasurer, or to any of the clergymen of the town, who will, no doubt, apply it to the desired purpose.

By acting thus we would be spared the time, so limited at present, considering the extraordinary pressure of duty upon us, as well as the pain of asking anything from towns-people, who are at all times so ready and generous in their contribution to charity. The objects of orignating the fund were – first, to prevent the recurrence of the inhuman spectacles which we witnessed, of BURYING THE DEAD WITHOUT COFFINS; and next, to secure the people of the town from being imposed upon by persons who, perhaps, had no one at all dead, calling for aid towards the price of a coffin or who, if they had, might misapply the money they received. In any case, the towns-people have been relieved from applications of this nature, and on this account as also on the account of humanity, each person – who can at all afford it – ought to give a little.

From this fund, about ten days in existence, ELEVEN destitute families, have been enabled to get coffins for their dead relations, and in each case of these there would have been a collection, from door to door, in the town, or else the remains of these persons would have continued a long time unburied, to the great danger of the community; or be carried to the grave in a manner disgraceful to the town and horrifying to the feelings of humanity.

May I take the liberty, then of requesting of you to call the attention of the towns-people to the suggestions here made? – I have the honour to be, your obedient servant.

MICHAEL CURLEY, R.C.C., Castlebar.

The following to a copy of Mr. Gibbons' letter:–

Westport, 11th Feb., 1847.

My Dear Mr. Curley – Having heard that, amongst the many other charitable acts of yours, you were making a collection for providing coffins for the remains of your destitute poor, pray accept the enclosed pound note from – Your very sincerely attached and obedient servant.

JOHN GIBBONS.

Tyrawly Herald (21-1-1847).

The Colony, Dugort.

ACHILL

For the relief of the sick, the very aged and the infirm – in Hospital, attending the Dispensary, and those visited in their cabins – I have not received one penny since March commenced, although never more required! and have only to acknowledge a donation of five Bags of Rice from the Central Relief Committee of the Society of Friends for which I am very thankful. By an order "from a constant friend" on Rev. W. B. Stoney's manufactory for giving employment to the poor of Castlebar – I have lately received seven comfortable freize frock coats for Patients recovering from fever, and I beg to earnestly recommend this class of sufferers to the benevolent; many may daily be seen tottering on their emaciated limbs in a state of almost nudity. Three frock coats can be had as above for 11.5s.

Post-office orders on Newport-Mayo, is by far the more safe and ready mode of transmitting donations.

For the Windows and Orphans of the 19 men drowned at Keele, I have received from I. Wood, Esq., H.M. ship, Boadicia, a collection amounting to 1l. 1s. 6d.; A Taylor, Esq., 14s. 2d.; John Drummond, Esq., 1l.; Irish Evangelist Society, 5l.; Miss Allingham, 5s.; Lady R. Boyle, 1l.; Miss Todd, 2s. 6d.; S. G. Claremons, 5s.; Mrs. E., per Robert Wyon, Esq., 1l. These poor Widows are now busily employed preparing the land for Three Ton of Potatoes, and one of seed Rye, under the care of an overseer.

NEASON ADAMS, M.D.

**Achill Missionary Herald
(March-1848).**

PARTRY CURATE

An unexpected invitation to visit the parish of Partra, by the active Catholic curate who resided there, was accepted. "You will find him," a protestant gentleman remarked, "an active honourable man among the poor, and one who has done much good." The country about him scarcely had a parallel, even in Skibbereen. Eleven miles from Castlebar opened a bright spot of taste – a glebe house and tidy new chapel, which this indefatigable curate had built in spite of all poverty. In the chapel were a few half-dead children huddled upon the floor, some around the altar, with their writing books upon the steps for desks, without table or benches. These the curate had gathered among the starving, for the sake of the black bread, which kept them barely alive.

This indefatigable man had caused a fever-shed to be erected, on a bog bordering upon the Lake of Musk, where pure air is circulating, and a snug cottage stands near, in which the matron who keeps the hospital resides. Thirty invalids were here, mostly sick from the effects of hunger, with swollen legs, many of them past all hope. Far away from any inhabitant, this hospital, cottage, and their inmates stood, struggling to keep up the dying flame of life, only to suffer fresh and hopeless troubles. Solitary as this region everywhere is, it was once celebrated ground.

Asenath Nicholson (1848)

CLOTHING FOR BALLINA POOR

THE BRITISH ASSOCIATION: We are given to understand that this humane Association intend shortly to furnish with articles of clothing the vast numbers of poor children, who are now receiving from them daily rations of bread. This will be a most important benefit to the distressed young creatures, many of whom are at present, in want of sufficient raiment. Their pure hearts should glow with gratitude at this fresh proof of the concern entertained for their comforts by their generous benefactors.

Tyrawly Herald (20-4-1847).

TILLAGE AT BALLINA

Upon more than one occasion we deemed it our duty to point attention to the laudable exertions now being made by the Society of Friends to give employment to the labouring population, who otherwise would remain idle, and to bring under cultivation a portion of that land, which, for the last two years, was permitted to run waste. They have now 550 acres, some of them already tilled, and the rest in preparation for the reception of various crops, and so carefully and scientifically are all the necessary operations carried on, that this land will serve as a model farm for the surrounding districts. All the operations are under the superintendence of Mr. Vaughan, the able Practical Instructor, who has been appointed under Lord Clarendon's letter. He is thus enabled to give instructions on the ground to the persons employed. The land is taken in different localities, and the people seem most anxious and ready to carry into effect the advice and suggestions of the Instructor. Indeed, they plainly perceive that it is their interest to do so, as, by adopting his recommendations, the land will be made to produce four fold more than under the old and unprofitable system of cultivation.

It is to be hoped, that every facility will be afforded the Society of Friends in their benevolent labours, because by their instrumentality, if no impediment be thrown in the way, a new and profitable system of cultivation will be introduced into the country, and the object, for which the Practical Instructor has received his mission, will be fully carried out. The gratitude of the Agricultural portion of Irishmen is justly due to Lord Clarendon, the originator of this instructive movement – a movement, which if unanimously joined in, will confer more permanent benefits on the country, than a thousand high sounding but empty and useless political concessions.

Tyrawly Herald (20-4-1847).

WESTPORT INDUSTRIAL SOCIETY

TO THE EDITOR OF THE MAYO CONSTITUTION.

Sir – May I beg you will permit me to make your paper a medium not only of an acknowledgment of the generous contributions we have already received in aid of the funds of the Westport Trades Industrial Society, but also of an appeal to all the readers of that paper (and more particularly to that portion of them who live in Westport and its neighbourhood) in behalf of the same. Should you kindly do so, you will save us the trouble of calling on them one by one, and give them an opportunity of making their contributions in favour of the funds by acts of spontaneous generosity. Need I say our society labours but for the prosperity, the comfort, and independence of our poor, destitute fellow-creatures, irrespective of their religious creed or parish (I say of their religious creed or of their parish), as we give employment alike to the people of the neighbouring parishes, whether they may be Catholic, Protestant, or Dissenter, as to the inhabitants of Westport, and it is this generous principle that enables me now to state that we have at this moment many hundreds employed at fair wages in the parishes of Kilgeever, Aughagower, Kilmena, Islandeady, and some in Newport. I will now give you the names of the subscribers:–

From the good Count Strelitzki (who may be truly styled one of the best and most disinterested friends of the Irish poor) … … … … … … …£330-0-0.

for which we return him a certain quantity of clothes for the poor.

Very Rev. Dean Burke …5-0-0.
Dominick W. Kearns … …1-0-0.
Patrick McGreal … … …1-0-0.
Philip Hastings … … …1-0-0.
John Corrigan … … … …1-0-0.
Mrs. O'Maley … … … …1-0-0.
John Waldron … … … …1-0-0.
John Coen … … … … …1-0-0.
Walter Burke … … … …1-0-0.
Central Relief Committee … … … …20-0-0.
Thady Gorman … … …1-0-0.
Dennis Burns … … … …1-0-0.
Captain Primrose … … …1-0-0.
Patrick Hogan … … … …1-0-0.
Per Rev. Dean Burke … …1-0-0.

Statement of the General Distribution of Seeds during the season 1848, purchased for this purpose by the Central Relief Committee of the Society of Friends.

COUNTIES.	TURNIP.			CARROT.			PARSNIP.			CABBAGE.		
	lbs. distributed.	Acres sown.	Persons supplied.	lbs. distributed.	Acres sown.	Persons supplied.	lbs. distributed.	Acres sown.	Persons supplied.	lbs. distributed.	Acres sown.	Persons supplied.
Armagh -- --	256	72	696	51	12½	261	28	5½	160	21	5	150
Carlow -- --	62	15	40									
Cavan -- --	903	157	1,264	126	22¼	662	57	12	304	10	2	127
Clare -- --	1,512	237¾	1,020	13	1½	30	10	1¼	40	141	35	485
Cork -- --	18,678¾	8,729	8,643	804	106¾	1,849	608	87	1,216	478	120	1,068
Donegal -- --	8,390	1,875½	8,868	518½	78¼	1,530	273½	49	1,289	381¾	70¾	788
Dublin -- --	240	60	85	40	6½	80						
Fermanagh -- --	2,231½	461	2,554	212	54	800	84	21	310	73	73	292
Galway -- --	18,860¾	4,285¼	17,295	841	117¾	2,405	869½	125	2,901	504¾	139½	3,794
Kerry -- --	2,190	516	1,486	20	5	182	20	5	182	20	5	51
Kildare -- --	111	24½	61	—	—	—	2	½	3	13	1½	5
Kilkenny - --	432	96¼	141	12½	2	12						
King's County --	2,308	480½	1,660	24	6	100	48	14	200	20	5	160
Leitrim -- --	5,247	1,143¾	6,406	197	34	731	204	45½	608	379	61¼	2,193
Limerick -- --	1,446½	357	1,664	80	11	100				145	36	580
Longford -- --	290	61	281	28	7	41	40	10½	81	7	1¼	36
Mayo -- --	31,062	7,446½	29,500	1,452½	349¼	5,123	1,027	252¼	3,782	1,017	219	4,763
Monaghan -- --	474	115	1,369	83	30½	524	112	14¼	613	6	2	60
Queen's County --	220	45	97									
Roscommon -- --	5,950	1,180¼	6,167	789	79	1,477	586	79¼	1,609	176	26½	1,882
Sligo -- --	3,344	685	1,747	276	36	787	254	33½	633	212	53	570
Tipperary -- --	2,173½	446	1,530	187	31¼	188	84	15½	78	79	20½	339
Westmeath -- --	1,540	313	1,227	40½	9	198	54	13	192	49½	7	297
Wexford -- --	492	106	279	24	3½	64	32	6½	59	8	8	128
	108,414	28,908¼	94,080	5,819	1,003	17,144	4,393	790½	14,260	3,741	891¼	17,768

Messrs. John and
   Eneas McDonnell ... ...2-0-0.
John Ludden   ... ...1-0-0.
John Eagan ... ...1-0-0.
John Guff   ... ...1-0-0.
Pat Stone   ... ...1-0-0.
Francis Woodhouse ... ...1-0-0.
Anthony Ruby   ... ...0-10-0.
W. Duke ... ...0-5-0.
Charles Hall   ... ...0-1-0.
John Wade ... ...1-0-0.
The Messrs. Graham ... ...5-0-0.

With the greatest gratitude I acknowledge the above subscriptions in aid of the funds of the Westport Industrial Society, and am, sir, yours, sincerely,

THOMAS O'DOWD,

**Presbytery, Westport,
10th August, 1849.**

CASTLEBAR CLERGY

The town of Castlebar has suffered much from the effects of the late Famine, the industry of its inhabitants having been paralysed by the cessation of all demand from the surrounding country. To obviate as much as possible the misery resulting from this, a society was organised by a number of benevolent individuals in the town, of whom Messrs. Curley and Gerraghty, the Roman Catholic curates, took the lead. They purchased a quantity of wool, and then employed the different artisans of the town in spinning, weaving, dyeing, shaping, and sewing it into suits of clothing. Upwards of one-hundred individuals, representing several hundreds of the population of the place, have thus received constant employment at their several occupations during a time when the natural sources of employment have been in abeyance. Excellent suits of frieze clothing (five-hundred of which have been purchased by Count Strelitzki for distribution in some other distressed part of the country) can be supplied for 10s. the suit. When these are sold, the original subscribed fund will be repaid, and the society enabled to continue their benevolent scheme, should the necessity of the time still require it.

James Caird (1850)

Tragedy at Doolough

One of the most infamous occurrences in County Mayo during the Famine happened in March of 1849, in the Louisburgh area. The circumstances of the event, which needlessy compelled many starving people to walk twenty miles or more, gives testimony to the callous and uncaring attitude of some officials charged with administering the Poor Law. The tragedy has long lived in the minds of the people of the Louisburgh area and is now commemorated annually by the Famine Walk, from Louisburgh to Delphi.

TO THE EDITOR OF THE MAYO CONSTITUTION.

Louisburgh,
April 5th, 1840.

Sir – On last Friday, 30th ult., Colonel Hogrove, one of the vice guardians of Westport union, and Captain Primrose, the poor law inspector, arrived here on that morning for the purpose of holding an inspection on the paupers who were receiving outdoor relief in this part of the union, but, from some cause or other, they did not, but started off immediately for Delphi Lodge. In a short time after, the relieving officer ordered the poor creatures forthwith to follow him to Delphi Lodge, as he would have them inspected early on the following morning, Saturday, 31st; and in obedience of this humane order, hundreds of these unfortunate living skeletons, men, women and children, might have been seen struggling through the mountain passes and roads for the appointed place. The inspection took place in the morning, and I have been told that nothing could equal the horrible appearance of those truly unfortunate creatures, some of them without a morsel to eat, and others exhausted from fatigue, having travelled upwards of 16 miles to attend the inspection.

It is not for me to say why the inspection took place at Delphi, it being the most remote part of the union, and some of the poor, as I have before stated, having to travel upwards of sixteen miles.

I have now the melancholy duty of informing you and the public, that a woman named Dalton, from Wastelands, six miles to the West of this town, her son and daughter, were all found dead on the road side, on

Delphi Lodge.

the morning after the inspection, midway between this town and Delphi: and about one mile nearer to this town, two men were found dead – in all, five. The bodies of these ill-fated creatures lay exposed on the road side for three or four days and nights, for the dogs and ravens to feed upon, until some charitable person had been buried in a turf hole at the road side.

Now, Sir, I call upon you, as the sincere friend of the poor, and in the name of that just God who is to judge all at the last day, to call upon the Lord Lieutenant of this county to demand a searching inquiry into this melancholy affair, and prevent, if possible, so many of the poor being sacrificed. If inquests are held, I will let you know the result. –

I am, Sir, your obedient servant,

A RATEPAYER.

Mayo Constitution (10-4-1849).

DOOLOUGH

TO THE EDITOR OF THE MAYO CONSTITUTION

Louisburgh, April 13th, 1849.

Sir – In my letter of the 5th instant, I attempted giving you an account of the first loss of life which took place in this part of the country, on the night of the 31st ultimo. I have this day the melancholy day of informing you that two more miserable creatures were found on the mountain passes dead – in all 7, and I am confidently informed that 9 or 10 more have never reached their homes, and several of those that did, were so fatigued with cold and hunger that they in a short time ceased to live. Gracious God! will my Lord Lucan, as Lieutenant of this county, suffer such extraordinary and cruel conduct to pass without a deep and searching inquiry, and to punish those who dare to sport with the lives of the people.

I tell Colonel Hogrove, and Captain Primrose that the relieving officer ordered the poor creatures to follow them to Delphi, in order that they might be inspected at 7 o'clock on the morning of the 31st, at that lodge, and I challenge them to contradict what I state; further that the cause of their not stopping at Louisburgh was, that the relieving officer had not his books ready, and it was at the court-house the following order was given – all persons not attending at 7 or 8 o'clock in the morning, at Delphi, would be struck off the relief; the people did attend, but the relieving officer did not until 12 o'clock.

I now think it right to inform you that a strictly private inquest was held by Mr. Coroner Burke, aided and assisted by a member of his family. Doctor Burke, who is the poorhouse doctor, and the jury returned the following verdict, after a post mortem examination on the bodies of two of them:– "Died from starvation and cold," when instead of providing coffins for those creatures, the bodies were again thrown into a mountain slough, with a few sods thrown over them immediately after.

The Coroner and his staff proceeded to Delphi Lodge, and on the following day returned and held another inquest; like verdict was returned, when the Coroner and doctor returned to their mansions, leaving three more unfortunate creatures at the road side, with scarce a covering of sods upon them.

Thank God all are not so hardened as the above, for that excellent and humane clergyman. I mean the Rev. Thomas O'Dowd, the Catholic Curate, gave five coffins to Mr. Walshe, who, to his credit be it said, both himself and his men had all the bodies taken out of the sloughs on the 12th instant, and placed in coffins, and had them respectably interred to a burial place.

It is much to be regretted that both Mr. Moroney, R.M.; Mr. Garvey, J.P., and Mr. Walshe

did not attend, if they did, I am certain that they would not sanction hole-and-corner inquests to be held. Why not examine witnesses who would prove who issued the inhuman order to follow their honours to Delphi Lodge? I tell both the coroner and his staff, as well as the guardians, that, a deep and searching inquiry shall and must be held, and show those gentlemen that they cannot sport with the lives of the poor in this part of the country.

Now, sir, will you believe it, that the relieving officer will take no applications for relief from any persons in this town or neighbourhood, but obliges the creatures to go to the village of Cregganebane, a distance of at least six miles, before he placed their names on the relief book, and then his honour must be followed to Westport.

I will now leave the matter in your hands, knowing you to be the sincere and steady friend of the poor. In my last, I stated that the poor had not to travel more than 10 or 15 miles, I now tell you that the residence of some of those found dead was at least 28 miles from Delphi – the same distance back.

I am, Sir,

Your obedient servant,

A RATEPAYER.

I omitted giving you the names of the persons found dead – Catherine Dillon, Patt Dillon and Honor Dillon, mother, son and daughter, living two-and-a-half miles from this town. Catherine Grady and Mary McHale of Wastelands, 10 miles from this; James Flynn of Rinnacully, 13 miles; so that instead of receiving their rations of the 30th – the day they expected it – in this town, they had to proceed on to Delphi Lodge, without a morsel to eat, a distance of at least fourteen miles. Furthermore, unless some steps be taken, I fear much that ere one month many a poor creature will meet the same fate.

Mayo Constitution (17-5-1849).

The Workhouse

Under the Poor Law Act of 1838, County Mayo was divided into five areas or unions; Ballina, Ballinrobe, Castlebar, Swinford and Westport. Each was managed by a Board of Guardians, which was required to maintain a workhouse, where paupers could be housed and fed. The Mayo unions covered a very large area, which compelled some seeking relief to walk several miles to the nearest workhouse. During the Famine, these workhouses soon became overwhelmed by those seeking admission. In 1849, the number of unions in Mayo was increased with the establishment of Belmullet, Claremorris, Killala and Newport unions.

BALLINROBE WORKHOUSE

In Ballinrobe the workhouse is in the most awfully deplorable state, pestilence having attacked paupers, officers, and all. In fact, this building is one horrible charnel house, the unfortunate paupers being nearly all the victims of a fearful fever, the dying and the dead, we might say, huddled together. The master has become the victim of this dread disease; the clerks, a young man whose energies were devoted to the well-being of the union, has been added to the victims; the matron, too, is dead; and the respected, and esteemed physician has fallen before the ravages of pestilence, in his constant attendance on the diseased inmates.

This is the position of the Ballinrobe house, every officer swept away, while the number of deaths among the inmates is unknown; and we forgot to add that the Roman Catholic chaplain is also dangerously ill of the same epidemic. Now the Ballinrobe board have complied with the Commissioner's orders, in admitting a houseful of paupers and in striking a new rate, which cannot be collected; while the unfortunate inmates, if they escape the awful epidemic, will survive only to be the subjects of a lingering death by starvation!

We have heard also of the inmates of the Westport workhouse and several of the officers being attacked by fever, but unfortunately without any fatal results. Ballina and Swinford, too, have not escaped the dreadful contagion, and Sligo has been fearfully scourged. The master – for many years a color-sergeant of the 88th regiment, who fought through many a bloody field unscathed – has fallen before dire disease, and the paupers are dying in dozens.

Mayo Constitution (23-3-1847)

CASTLEBAR WORKHOUSE

Mr. Gibbons to Mr. Redington
Castlebar,
January 8, 1847.

I beg leave most respectfully to submit, for the consideration of the Lord-Lieutenant, the state of the poor-house of this Union. It is, unhappily, too

Names of Unions, arranged in Provinces and Counties, according to the Situation of each Workhouse.	Total No. of Paupers for which Accommodation is provided in each Union.	Number of Paupers in each Workhouse.								Total Number of Deaths within the periods stated.	Average Weekly Cost of Maintenance per Head, exclusive of Clothing.
		Able-bodied			Sick.			All other Classes.	Total Number in Workhouse.		
		Male.	Female.	Total.	Fever Cases.	Other Cases.	Total.				
County of MAYO:—											
Ballina . . . Sat. 9 Jan. 1847	1,200	24	114	137	..	130	130	762	1,029	25	2 0
,, ,, 10 Jan. 1846	..	17	19	36	..	80	80	232	348	..	1 10¼
,, ,, 11 Jan. 1845	..	16	16	32	..	66	66	222	320	..	1 7
Ballinrobe . . . ,, 9 Jan. 1847	800	15	115	130	..	30	30	552	712	11	1 8
,, ,, 10 Jan. 1846	..	3	3	6	..	14	14	77	97	..	1 9
,, ,, 11 Jan. 1845	..	3	3	6	..	10	10	75	91	..	1 5
Castlebar . . . ,, 9 Jan. 1847	600	2	8	10	..	21	21	92	123	..	2 0
,, ,, 10 Jan. 1846	..	4	11	15	..	15	15	77	107	..	1 8
,, ,, 11 Jan. 1845	..	4	9	13	..	15	15	65	93	..	1 3¼
Swineford . . . ,, 9 Jan. 1847	700	22	87	109	8	103	111	473	693	3	1 11½
,, ,, 10 Jan. 1846	not open.										
,, ,, 11 Jan. 1845											
Westport . . . ,, 9 Jan. 1847	1,000	62	107	169	2	36	38	334	541	2	1 8¼
,, ,, 10 Jan. 1846	..	2	17	19	2	3	5	47	71	..	1 5
,, ,, 11 Jan. 1845	..	..	..	..	..	..	..	..	..	..	..

Return for week ended 9th January, 1847 (Parliamentary Papers)

well known by the reports of local journals transcribed into the public papers, that the house is closed against the admission of paupers during the present trying visitation on the poor, but the condition of those confined in the house, upwards of 100, is not generally known. I am a frequent visitor of the workhouse; after inspecting each class of the inmates, and I am pained to have to state that almost every individual of the 100 or more are showing striking signs of haggard and famished looks; the provisions, oaten or Indian meal, is supplied very irregularly, often not sent to the house until an advanced hour of the day, in quantities of 200 lbs. or so, but never in a large or satisfactory supply. Turf is most irregularly supplied; on many days not all

sent, the cause of having the breakfast meal deferred to one or two o'clock, p.m. On New Year's Day the paupers had only one diet, and that at a late hour. The master states that he is obliged to permit the paupers to continue in their beds for heat's sake.

The hospital is occupied by the old men, and the children pining away by hunger and cold. Coffins with difficulty procured for those who die. They are prevented by their sufferings from attending the instructions they would otherwise receive from an excellent master, and an equally competent schoolmistress.

I beg to pray that his Excellency be assured that I do not exaggerate the deplorable state of this district, Castlebar Workhouse, and that rather, perhaps, I have to blame

myself that I did not make this communication to you, Sir, earlier. I had thought the Poor Law Commissioners might have secured the good treatment of the few confined in the house, though they could not compel or enforce the admission of others; the contrary is almost the case; those who are able to creep are preferring to brave want abroad to dying by cold and hunger inside. I again take leave to pray that this lamentable, but true state of the poor-house, Castlebar Union district, be submitted to the Lord Lieutenant.

Parliamentary Papers (1847)

BALLINA WORKHOUSE

LIEUT. HAMILTON
to the COMMISSIONERS:
December 5, 1847.

WITH reference to my letter of yesterday's date, in which I stated that 300 paupers were to be removed yesterday from the workhouse to the store, which a Committee of the Guardians had taken in the morning, I beg to acquaint you that notwithstanding the greatest exertions on the part of the officers of the workhouse, it was found impracticable to move them earlier than this day; consequently 1698 person had to be provided for last night in the workhouse.

I was at the workhouse early today, and had every possible precaution taken against infection.

The applicants for admission are in the most miserable and filthy state; there is neither bedding nor clothing for 600.

I am now going to see the Chairman of the Board, with the view of summoning a special meeting of the Guardians.

I must say, I think that the Guardians ought to have been earlier prepared. On the 8th

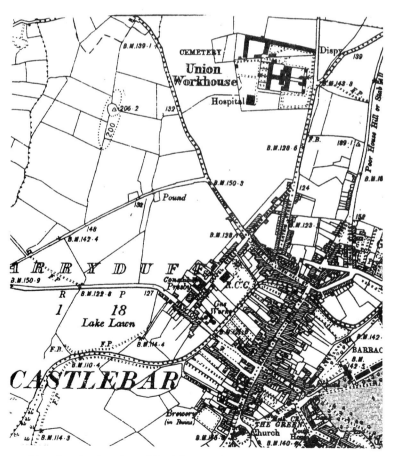

Map showing location of Castlebar Workhouse based on the Ordnance Survey, by permission of the Government *(Permit No.: 6407)*.

November, I requested them to make arrangements for giving outdoor relief to persons legally entitled to it, but this step was deferred until it was too late to be of any use. Unless the Board meet more frequently, and give more time to business, it is impossible that they can carry on the business of this large Union properly.

MR. DEVLIN
to LIEUT. HAMILTON:
December 10, 1847.
I AM just now returned from visiting the patients in the infirmary. They are suffering much, in consequence of the numbers that are crowded into it.

I have no hesitation in saying that, unless additional accommodation be procured for the sick, many lives will be sacrificed; indeed, in order to keep the house in a healthy state, several hundreds of the present inmates ought to be removed; and may I beg that you will call the attention of the Guardians to this subject.

Parliamentary Papers (1848)

BALLINROBE WORKHOUSE

THE REV. MR. PHEW
to the COMMISSIONERS:
January 8, 1848.
I beg to state for the infor-mation of the Poor Law Commissioners, that the poor starving people of this electoral Shrule division are almost neglected by the Vice-Guardians of this Union. About three or four-hundred of the most destitute families of this division have crawled to Ballinrobe (a distance of 10 or 12 miles), every Friday for the last month, seeking admission to the workhouse or out-door relief. This I can certify, for I have accompanied the poor creatures thither in order to represent their wants to the

BALLINA UNION.

A SCHOOLMASTER WANTED.

 THE VICE GUARDIANS of the above Union will on SATURDAY, the 13th October inst., proceed to appoint a competent person to fill the situation of

S C H O O L M A S T E R,

TO THE BALLINA UNION WORKHOUSE.
At a salary of £25 per annum, with the usual Rations and Apartments.

None need apply who is not fully qualified to discharge officially the duties of the office. A person acquainted with the National System of Education would be preferred.

Application (addressed to the Vice Guardians, accompanied by Testimonials as to character and competency) will be received by me at the Workhouse, up to 10 o'Clock a.m. on the above-named day, when candidates are requested to be in attendance.

By Order,
P. M·NULTY.
Clerk of the Union.
Board Room, Workhouse, Oct. 2, 1849.

Ballina Union notice

Guardians; and yet, though they remained each day until night, standing in wet and cold at the workhouse door, craving for admission into the house, they have got no relief and I do now most solemnly assure you that, but for a few shillings which I used to distribute to buy bread to enable their poor families to return home very many of them would have died by the road-side whilst returning from Ballinrobe. Six poor creatures who have been dragged to Ballinrobe in this manner, have died in this electoral division this week, and I am greatly afraid that treble that number will meet the same awful death before this day week.

I also beg to call the Commissioners' particular attention to the fact that there is no relieving officer resident in this electoral division. The Gentleman, Mr. Charles T. Carr, who is the relieving officer for this division, has also upon his shoulders two other electoral divisions, viz., Kilmain and Kilmolara, and resides not in any one of the three electoral divisions, but in Ballinrobe; he is not even allowed to spend one hour in each week in this electoral division. So far from visiting the residences of the applicants for relief, not a single cabin has he visited since his appointment, save the cabin where a coroner's inquest had been held on the body of John Toole, who was found dead by the road side on his return from the Ballinrobe Union workhouse, whither he had gone on Friday, the 31st December, to seek admission to the workhouse or out-door relief, and died same night. This plainly shows the necessity of a resident relieving officer in each electoral division. Mr. Carr is not to blame; he has as much duty imposed on him as six could not adequately attend to; besides, it is no saving whatever to the Union; on the contrary, because, when the relieving officer is not resident, and goes not to visit the residences of the applicants for relief, there is no check on imposition. I have been informed that two families from the Galway Union have imposed on him, by stating they were from this electoral division, and have been rationed and received rations.

Parliamentary Papers (1848)

WESTPORT WORKHOUSE

MR. LYNCH
to the COMMISSIONERS:
March 15th, 1848.
I HAVE the honour to report for the information of the Poor Law Commissioners, that the number of persons applying for relief during the past week

A scene at the gate of a workhouse during the Famine.

has been much smaller than usual. I attribute this reduction to the large number of applicants in the previous week, who were offered in-door instead of outdoor relief. The number on the out-door list is about the same as it was last week, for though the Vice-Guardians added this day 333, there were 265 taken off, independent of those who will be struck off on Friday, for no attendance at work.

There are now a very large number of stout able-bodied men in the workhouse and they created serious alarm this morning by refusing to go to their ordinary work, alleging that they did not get enough of food; but their real motive was to be put on the out-door relief. I made inquiry and find that these men get two meals in the day, with a small allowance of either milk or molasses, while those on the out-door relief receive but one pound per day of raw meal.

On being made acquainted with the turbulent state of the house, I directed a list of the most prominent actors to be made out, and from this list I selected 28 who were either single men, or being married, had not more than two persons depending on them, and upon their admitting before me and one of the Vice-Guardians that they refused to work, we had them at once discharged from the house, and having intimated to the other paupers, that the same course would be adopted in every case where the able-bodied refused to work, the other men went most obediently to their work, and order was thus restored.

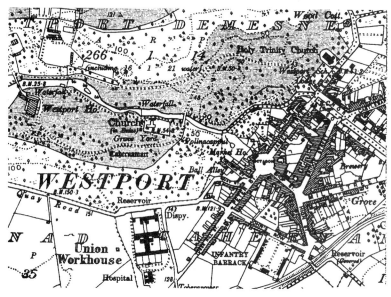

Map showing location of Westport Workhouse, based on the Ordnance Survey, by permission of the Government (*Permit No. 6407*).

Parliamentary Papers (1848)

SWINFORD WORKHOUSE

MR. GIBBONS
to the COMMISSIONERS:
March 25, 1848.

I BEG to state that the Union-house required my unremitting attention during the past week.

The master and porter being both ill of fever, and there being neither schoolmaster nor mistress, has caused considerable relaxation of discipline in the house.

On the 23rd instant I counted all the inmates in every part of the house, including the infirmary and fever wards, etc., and found the total number amounted to 373 individuals, including all ages, being a very considerable decrease from the number stated in the weekly return.

I have had the names, ages, and parish of all now in the house taken down, with the view of inquiring into the cause of the decrease, and ascertaining if any parties have left the house without authority, and whether the full number stated in the weekly return was actually in the house.

There are not at present more than six able-bodied men in

SWINFORD UNION.
NOTICE
To Building Contractors.

THE Board of Guardians of the above Union will on TUESDAY, the 6th day of APRIL next, receive and consider Tenders to

BUILD A FEVER HOSPITAL

on the Workhouse ground, to accommodate 60 Patients, according to the Plan and Specification to be seen on application to me at my Office, in the Swineford Workhouse.

Sealed Tenders, addressed to the Chairman of the Board of Guardians, stating therein the sum required for the whole Building, and the latest day on which the contract will be completed, will be received by me up to 11 o'clock, A.M., on the above date.

The names and addresses of two solvent sureties, with the proposer, as security, to be inserted in each tender.

By Order,
RICHARD KYLE, Clerk of the Union.
Poor Law Office, Swineford,
March 24th, 1847.

Swinford Union notice.

the house; the great majority of those returned as able-bodied are boys over or at 15 years, and few of those are able-bodied.

There were several able-bodied men in the house last week, but they discharged themselves, and many of them have left for England, as I am informed.

The work I had in progress of deepening the drains is all stopped for want of assistance.

I should mention that many of the paupers have left the house on account of the master and porter being in fever, and I have constant communications, stating that those who have left the house have caused fever and other

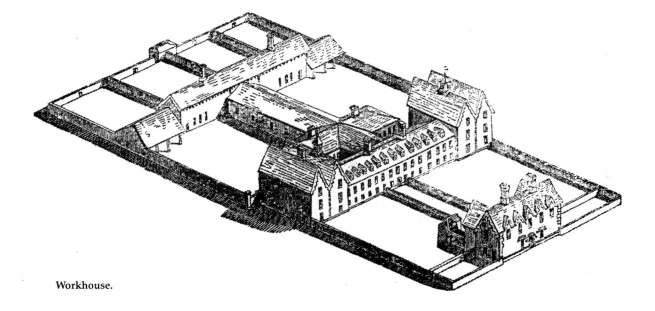

Workhouse.

Interior of a workhouse.

sickness to spread through the Union.

All the destitute admitted for relief this last week have been allowed one week of out-door on account of the fever being in the house and the insufficiency of clothing, also to have the old clothing cleaned and repaired, and to have the probationary wards whitewashed, etc., etc.

I have directed that the relieving officers should send in a return of all the able-bodied persons on their books, distinguishing them in classes; also a return of the number of women whose husbands are stated to be in England, as this class is excessive of this Union.,

I have before reported it as my opinion that had the Visiting Committee attended to their duty, the house could not have fallen into the present state of neglect, respecting clothing, the absence of all discipline, as well as the filthy state of the probationary wards and other parts of the premises.

Parliamentary Papers (1848)

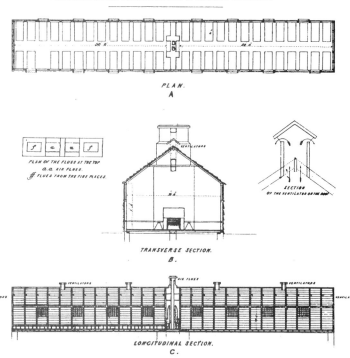

PLAN AND SECTIONS OF TEMPORARY FEVER WARDS
OF ECONOMICAL CONSTRUCTION
FOR **50** PATIENTS,
PREPARED FOR THE CENTRAL BOARD OF HEALTH IRELAND.

Crimes of Desperation

The incidence of crime rose during the Famine. Most involved the theft of food and were carried out in desperation. There were also attacks on rent and rate collectors. Fifteen thousand extra troops were drafted to police the country and new laws were enacted.

ACHILL PLUNDER

We regret extremely to state that a hooker belonging to General Thompson, of Connemara, which put into Achill Sound, at the south of the island, from stress of weather, was plundered by a party of the natives of this island. One person suspected of being concerned in this outrage has been apprehended, and there is reason to hope that others also will be brought to justice. We tell the natives of Achill, and they know that the advice is given by a real friend, that any man among them who engages in such lawless proceedings is the enemy of the whole population. The general good conduct of our poor islanders under their distressing trial is deserving of the highest commendation; the lawless conduct of some to which we have alluded is the

only exception. We trust that there will be no repetition of it. Our appeals on their behalf have been enforced by reference to the exemplary patience with which they endured their trials, and if some evil-minded persons are permitted to pervert the general distress into an occasion for breaking the laws of God and man, we shall be deprived of the most powerful plea we had to advance in applying to those who have both the means and the inclination to relieve them.

Achill Missionary Herald (January-1847).

SHEEP STEALING

John Gennelly was indicted with having stole, in the month of December last, a sheep, the property of Robert Carey, of Erris.

The charge having been fully

proved, Mr. T. W. Kelly, who defended the prisoner, admitted, that he did take the sheep in day light, but as he was starving, he contended that it was no robbery and that he was actionable for the value of the sheep.

Mr. Kelly then proceeded to address the Jury on behalf of the prisoner. He said: – Gentlemen, there is no one who reprobates or condemns crime more than I do, and when you have a robber arraigned before you he should not be allowed to escape without due punishment. But it should be a crime that ought to be visited with punishment, and when judging on crime the intention and not the act is to be taken into consideration. This, I will show you in his worship's presence, who knows the law. I tell you that if the man was starving and came to the owner of the sheep, and said I'm starving and took a sheep, that act does not constitute the act of robbery, because he had not taken with a felonious intention. This poor man was steeped in misery, and what rendered his case worse, he beheld his wife and family starving around him. A man may suffer a great deal himself; he may bear patiently and without repining the pangs of hunger, but when he sees his wife and children without anything to eat and starving in his presence, he cannot stand it. Death in such a case would be preferable as it would be a release from suffering. There is a curse upon the country, but it is not the poor that have brought it on it; it is not this poor man who

Achill Sound.

An attack on a potato store.

has been the cause of it. The government are doing a good deal to relieve the existing distress, but if union and unanimity prevailed to a greater extent the people would not be starving. I conjure the poor people to be patient in their sufferings and to respect the laws, and I also conjure the rich to share out of their abundance with the poor, who are formed of the same materials with themselves, for in proportion as they will divide with them here in the distress, in the same proportion will they be rewarded in another place. Gentlemen, I shall now leave my client in your hands, conscious that you will weigh well the true state of his case, and that you will not confound him with the common herd of robbers.

The jury, after the lapse of some short time, brought in a verdict of guilty, and the Barrister, when about passing sentence, said that the court having taken into consideration the extreme destitution of the prisoner, would only inflict on him three months' imprisonment and hard labour.

Tyrawly Herald (21-1-1847).

WESTPORT MOB

On the night of Monday last, or morning of Tuesday, a mob broke open the store of M. McDonnell, Esq., Westport, and took therefrom seven barrels of flour, which they divided amongst themselves at the door, leaving the empty barrels behind them. The watchman on the premises, whom they overpowered, could not recognise any of the plunderers.

The guardians of the Westport Union had come to the decision of closing the Workhouse on Monday last, but Lord Sligo

most humanely interfered and guaranteed to supply the house for three weeks, till the intention of government was known.

Tyrawly Herald (21-1-1847).

MURDER AT DOWNPATRICK

We are informed that a brutal murder was perpetrated a few days ago at a place called Castletown, close to Downpatrick, within about four miles of Ballycastle in this county. The victim was a poor old widow, named Mary Hegarty, 75 years of age. The house in which she resided was detached from the others in the village, and on the day of the murder, she was quite alone, some members of her family having gone to the shoreside for the purpose of gathering seaweed for food, and another having repaired to Ballycastle in order to get some soup. The poor woman had a small bag of meal in the house, and this circumstance being known to a boy, named James, who lived in the same locality, he determined to avail himself of the absence of her family and to rob her of the meal. He accordingly went to the widow's house, and either to effect his purpose, or to prevent discovery, he inflicted six or seven desperate wounds on her

Downpatrick Head and Dunbrista.

head with a loy which he found in the house. He then seized on the bag of meal, and just as he was leaving the house with his bloody booty another boy, belonging to the village, happened to be passing by, and seeing the old woman weltering in her gore, he, at once, thought that all was not right and immediately pursued the murderer and robber. Having overtaken him he took the bag of meal from him and, of course, identified him.

At the inquest the jury returned a verdict of wilful murder against James, who absconded, but, who, it is to be hoped, will shortly be made amenable to justice.

Tyrawly Herald (13-4-1847).

BLACKSOD BAY – PIRACY

It again becomes our painful duty to state that piratical attacks on trading vessels have not in the least abated on the Erris coast. On Monday, the fourth instant, a vessel called the Kate Thorn, Andrew McWhenny, Master, on her way to Newport from Liverpool freighted with American flour, Indian corn and Indian meal, to Messrs. John Malley and son, was surrounded by ten boats off Eagle Island – each boat being manned by from six to ten persons. While the pirates were making vigorous preparations to board the object of their plunder a propitious breeze sprung up which bore the ship away from her rapacious pursuers. No cutter or other vessel was in sight, so that had these marauders effected boarding the vessel, plunder to an enormous extent, with loss of life, in case of resistance, would have been the inevitable consequence. We cannot too severely censure the conduct of the guard ships in the neighbourhood of Blacksod, for not using the most vigorous exertions to protect the property

Escorting a wagon of meal.

of merchants and others, engaged in the provision trade. We copy the following from the Daily News of the 7th instant: – "On Saturday the schooner Elizabeth and Mary, laden with oats, from Limerick to Glasgow, arrived at the Tail of the Bank, and reported that she had been boarded when off Blacksod Point, west of Ireland, by a banditti of from seventy to eighty fellows, who forcibly took away from 15 to 20 tons of the cargo." Where were her Majesty's armed vessels, said to be cruising along our coast?

The Telegraph (13-10-1847).

ATTEMPT TO PLUNDER A MEAL STORE

The increasing depravity of the times, particularly amongst the younger classes, and which the system of outdoor relief – administered as it is – tends greatly to increase, cannot more strongly be exemplified than in a case which came before the Petty Sessions of this town on Thursday last. Police Constable Carey, of Islandeady, who is charge of the meal store from which the relief is distributed in that union, having from time to

time missed quantities of the meal, and having examined the windows and locks found all secure. Still the meal vanished, as if by magic hands; at length he perceived a small quantity of soot on the floor – this gave him a clue to the theft, and on the same evening he brought the rest of his party into the store as if to inspect the meal, one of them, however, on retiring, was left unperceived by the people in the store, and the doors and windows were secured in the usual way. When it got some-what dusk the policeman heard a noise in the chimney, and a lad about 17 or 18 years of age slid quietly down and commenced filling his bag when, to his dis-may and horror, the policeman came forth from his concealment and seized upon his prey who, on the alarm, vainly attempted to ascend the chimney, but it would not do. It is believed that another was at the top of the chimney to draw up the bag, but who, quietly made his escape. What makes the thing worse is that this young robber's family was in the receipt of the relief, and they had, on the day previous, received 45 lbs. of meal, quite sufficient, it was proved, to meet their necessities. He was fully committed for trial.

Mayo Constitution (4-7-1848).

PLUNDER AT CURRANE

PLUNDER OF MEAL – On Thursday last, a boat laden with meal for the use of the children attending the schools, and of the poor in the Achill district, left Westport, in charge of a man named Gallagher, who, it appears, run her aground at Currane, where during the night she was attacked, and plundered of all the meal she contained, by upwards of one hundred men and women. Informations have been sworn against several of the robbers, most of whom are said to be above want, and who by their conduct, deprived thousands of the poor of that miserable district of a present supply of food. Doctor Dillon has issued warrants for the arrest of a number of persons against whom informations have been sworn.

Mayo Constitution (26-12-1848)

POLICE ESCORT AT SHEEANE

We have been told by a valued friend of ours that on Monday last M. McDonnell, Esq., despatched several cars laden with flour, under a police escort, from Westport to Castlebar. When they got some distance from Westport they found the roads crowded by country men and women, and to prevent any misfortune occurring the escort deemed it more prudent to return with the cars to that town

again. Mr. Barron, R.M., upon hearing of the circumstances rode out in the direction of Sheeane, and having satisfied himself of the fact he returned to Westport. We hope his report to the Government will be the means of obtaining speedy relief for the poor who are thus driven, as a last resource to keep soul and body together, on the Queen's high ways.

The Telegraph (13-1-1849).

ROBBING GARDENS

The potato fields in the neighbourhood of this town are nightly plundered by persons robbing and destroying the half-grown crops. We have reason to believe that many of these robberies are perpetrated by pauper urchins who escape at night from the auxiliary workhouses. The public are seriously damaged by this conduct, and proper caution should be used to prevent their recurrence. The guardians have expelled several paupers on charges of the above description, but this is only making matters worse.

Mayo Constitution (7-8-1849).

POLICE ROBBED

A Bangor correspondent of the Mayo Constitution states: "Sheep stealing is gone to such an extent in this part of the country that it is almost impossible for the farmer to keep any of his valuable stock.

Some nights ago, 9 prime sheep, the property of Mr. Daly of Doonacastle, were stolen. Two very fine sheep, purchased by the Constabulary at this place and put into a house convenient to the barrack were stolen while the party were out on patrol; it appears either through some alarm, or through fear, the thieves hid one of the sheep in a garden adjoining the barrack; the police, in making a seemingly careless search, found the carcase buried – where they let it remain; and the five following nights the party with their sergeant (Foster), a vigilant and active officer, kept due watch on the body of the sheep; about midnight, a notorious sheep stealer entered the garden, opened the hiding place, and took the sheep on his shoulders, when he was immediately apprehended, and brought before that active magistrate, Mr. Walsh, who immediately committed him for trial. It is anxiously hoped that at the next quarter sessions a few examples will be made.

Tyrawly Herald (15-2-1849).

GAOL

WINDOW SMASHING – The breaking of windows are become of daily occurrence in this town latterly. The object of those guilty of this offence is to get themselves committed to gaol, being starving while at large. Poor way this for wretched creatures to eke out existence.

The Telegraph (27-9-1849).

The County Gaol in Castlebar (Wynne Collection).

Fatal Endeavours

In efforts stave off the pangs of hunger, the people turned to whatever sources they could for sustenance. Turnips and imported maize were no substitute for the nutritious potato. Fishing at sea was hazardous, particularly in winter, in poorly maintained boats. For many, their endeavours had fatal consequences.

RECEIPTS FOR MAKING VARIOUS ARTICLES OF FOOD OF INDIAN CORN MEAL

CORN MEAL PUDDING – Scald four quarts of milk, stir into it one quart of sifted meal, one cup of molasses, a tablespoon of salt, a little spice of any kind you like; bake it three or four hours in pretty hot oven.

BUCK-WHEAT CAKES – This cheap article of food is considered a luxury throughout most of the American States, from 1st October to 1st of April. During this period, it is found almost everywhere at breakfast on the most frugal and most sumptuous tables. When eaten warm with butter, sugar, molasses, or treacle, it possesses a flavour, that cannot be equalled by any other griddle-cake whatever. – The buck-wheat flour put up in small cakes in Philadelphia, is the best that can be produced in America. – Recipe: Mix the flour with cold water; put in a little carbonate of soda; fry them the same as any griddle cakes. Leave enough of the batter to leaven the next mess. To be eaten with butter, molasses or sugar.

IMPROVED METHOD OF MAKING INDIAN STIRABOUT. – Two pounds of Indian meal put in three pints of boiling water, stir it very well, and then leave in steeped all night. In the morning, have ready three quarts of water in your stirabout pot on the fire when boiling, put in the Indian meal you have steeped, stir well, and when it has boiled for an hour, stir in a pound of oaten meal, and let it boil another half hour. This will give four able bodied men a good breakfast, and the cost is about 4½d.

Mayo Constitution (29-9-1846).

CARRION

TO THE EDITOR OF THE TYRAWLY HERALD.

A pig, having died of disease near Rappa Castle, was thrown into a dung-pit, and after remaining there for a few days became so offensive from decomposition, that it had to be placed in a deeper hole in the pit and covered. On the same evening, the mother of a large family, learning it was there, came after night set in and removed it. The remainder of the night she spent in cleaning and preparing it for her children, a most difficult task – I should say; as the smell from it, to use her own expression "was strong enough to knock down a horse." No wonder then – that disease should prevail to such an extent, and that the list of mortality should be so fearfully increased, when the majority of our poor people have no better food than what is suitable for pigs – and, failing even to procure that – are

RICE !
Rice ! Rice ! Rice !

ONE pound weight of whole RICE boiled with five quarts of Water, thickened with one pound weight of Oatmeal, make 8¼lbs of *beautiful* Food. The Rice to be put down first with one quart of water—the remaining four quarts of water to be added as the Rice swells; then put in the pound weight of Oatmeal, and stir all together. THIS DISH OF 8¼LBS. CAN BE HAD FOR SIX PENCE.

If the Rice be steeped for five or six hours it will be better. On trial it will be found that this dish of Stirabout will be made on *cheaper terms* than either Indian Meal or Oatmeal Stirabout, and preferable in quality to either.

¶ To be had *Wholesale* (in bags) at: JAMES FYNN'S, Victoria-Place, Galway. (3p)

Advert from Mayo Telegraph (10-2-1847)

A famine meal.

glad to eat the rotten swine. I am the more surprised at this

Gathering seaweed.

occurrence in the vicinity of Rappa Castle, as Annesley Knox, Esq., the benevolent and humane proprietor of that hospital mansion, not content with having already remitted to his numerous tenantry generally, a 'half year's (and) in many instances, a year's rent with arrears – feeds daily at his own house under the immediate superintendence of the amiable and charitable Mrs. Knox, upwards of 100 persons, with substantial soup and beef food. I would merely say to all whom God has blessed with affluence in this season of famine and distress – "go and do likewise."

Believe me, to remain, Mr. Editor,

Very faithfully, yours,

OBSERVER.
Ballina, 30th December, 1846.

Tyrawly Herald (31-12-1846).

SEAWEED

Portacloy is a deep rift in these hostile cliffs, otherwise wholly inaccessible for many miles. These is scarcely any proper landing, the beach being high and rough with rocks; and so great is the swell and turbulence of the ocean that accidents not unfrequently happen. A man had recently been swept off the rocks while catching crabs; and two poor women, we afterwards heard, met with the same fate that very morning, while gathering seaweed for food.

W. J. BENNETT (18-3-47)

FISHING

On the evening of the 8th inst. six boats of fishermen from the village of Keel went out, over a calm sea, to cast their nets for the night, when suddenly a storm of unusual violence came on, driving them from land to the ocean. One small canoe only returned in safety; one boat made the land at Dooega, the crew perished on the beach. I have just returned from the melancholy and afflicted village of Keel, where I made out the following list – of nineteen men drowned, leaving fourteen widows, and thirty-eight orphans. The Irish cry resounding from the cabins, the wild screaming of the orphans, and the tears of the aged, made it one of the most distressing sights I ever witnessed.

Achill Missionary Herald (November-1847).

BLACK BREAD

Last week we drew 'attention to the abominable stuff in the shape of bread distributed to the recipients of outdoor relief, in return for which they are required to break stones by the way side. We did so, not for the purpose of bringing on their heads the well deserved odium, for their convenience at such scandalous inhumanity; but we were actuated by the desire that our exposure might cause the distribution of this food to be disappointed in this expectation – still the noxious food is given as the only sustenance of hundreds, and our worst fears are being realised, for dysentery and fever are rapidly spreading amongst the persons supported by this relief. At this moment dozens of deaths may be traced to the use of this deleterious trash; and we are confident that a persistence in it will be productive of the greatest mortality. We could shock the public with numerous medical certificates of the destructive qualities of this black bread, and we think much credit is due the Surgeon of the Castlebar Dispensary for having combated with the officials on this important subject, and we trust

that if within his practice, a death ensue after his having given notice to the relieving officers of the dangerous use of this rye bread, that decided steps will be taken, that a court of justice may decide whether the paid guardians, or the inspecting or relieving officers, or any of them, are answerable for such death.

Mayo Constitution (4-4-1848).

GRASS

FATAL INDUSTRY – We, last week, had to record the death of a poor creature who expired near Westport, from actual hunger, a quantity of grass being the only substance in his stomach. When we chronicled his death amongst others, we, of course, never once imagined that he could have been what was once denominated a comfortable farmer; but such is the fact, the deceased held land in one of the distant islands, had actually planted half an acre of potatoes, sowed an acre of oats, which exhausted all his resources, and then he repaired to the mainland to seek for employ. He came to Westport Quay, looked for work in vain;

pledged his loy for one day's support; his shoes for a second; but alas! suffering from want had gone too far, and he fell the victim. Where then was the outdoor relief – for how far did he, once a ratepayer, benefit by the enormous humbug.

Mayo Constitution (24-4-1848).

SHELLFISH

On Monday, the 3rd April, four men and three women went out in a small Curragh, for the purpose of picking up seaweed, and shellfish, on a rock near the Island of Ennisglora, on the Erris coast. they remained on the rock for two hours; when returning, after getting the fish, etc., a heavy sea struck the Curragh and upset it. However, they got back to the rock safe where they had to remain all night, having no way of escape. On Tuesday, the 4th, two of the crew died of hunger and cold. On Wednesday two more died, and one was washed away and has not been since found. The other two, a man and woman, had to remain on the rock until Friday, without any nourishment, on which day they were taken off by the Coast Guards. The other four were lying dead on the rock all the time. On Monday, the 10th, Charles Atkinson, Esq., Coroner, held an inquest on the bodies when the above horrifying facts were elicited. The persons who remained alive were man and wife. Were it not for the attention of the Coast Guards they, too, would have perished, but they are now perfectly well.

Tyrawly Herald (13-4-1848).

DONKEYS

A Correspondent asks how is it to be accounted for that so many poor persons are now to be found in our streets carrying baskets of turf on their backs, for sale? Our answer is – the asses are nearly all dead, and consumed, we believe, as human food.

The Telegraph (5-4-1848).

BLACK BREAD

A school of 140 or 150 girls were in waiting for this bread, which had been sent for to the shop. It came, was cut in slices, and having been baked that morning, the effluvia was fresh, and though standing at the extremity of a long room, with the street door open, the nausea became so offensive that after taking a slice for a pattern, and having ascertained from the teacher that this was the daily bread which she had been cutting for weeks, I hastened home with the prize, placed the bread upon paper where good air could react it; the disagreeable smell gradually subsided, but the bread retained all its appearance for weeks, never becoming sour, but small spots of a greenish colour like mould here and there dotted up it. These spots were not abundant: the remainder appeared precisely like turf-mould, and was judged to be so.

Asenath Nicholson (1848)

NETTLES

Doctor Barrett, Superintendent of the Carra Dispensary, was last week called on to go see the poor man: upon entering the cabin he found him lying in a corner: asked what was the matter with him, when he replied, he, with his family, were dying from starvation. Upon further inquiry the doctor found the only food in the house to be some NETTLES! and about half-penny worth of flour, to mix thro' the nettle mash! On arriving in town Doctor Barrett related the result of his visit and inquiry to the Rev. Mr. Curley, R.C.C., who kindly handed him 2s. for the starving creatures. With this timely aid the doctor hastened on horseback to the residence of poor White. On his way thither, and within view of the cabin, he accosted Mr. Sheridan, the relieving officer, in company with Mr. Thomas Ford, of this town. He stated to them the object of his visit; requested of them both to accompany him, and see the poor man. They did so, and in their presence the doctor handed to the wretched victim of starvation the bounty of the Rev. Mr. Curley. The relieving officer, impressed with the misery of those in the cabin, promised to have immediate relief given them, but up to this no aid hath reached the miserable creatures. In the meantime the man has died. How long his family can survive will depend upon the NETTLES about the cabin.

The Telegraph (7-6-1848).

TURNIPS

When it was found that turnips could be so easily grown, and that no blast had as yet injured them, they were hailed with great joy by the peasants and by the people. But the starving ones soon found they were unsatisfactory, for when they had eaten much more in bulk than of the potato they were still craving, and the result was a pitiable sight to see them. No one thought it was the turnip: but I found in every place on the coast where they were fed on them the same results, and as far as I could ascertain, such died in a few weeks, and the rational conclusion must be, that a single root, so innutritious and so watery as the white turnips are, cannot sustain a healthy state of the system, nor life itself for any

The Curragh (From sketches by Charles Whymper).

Catastrophe for an evicted family.

considerable time. When going through the Barony of Erris, the appearance of these turnip-eaters became quite a dread. Invariably the same results appeared wherever used, and they became more to be dreaded, as it was feared the farmer would make them a substitute for the potato, and the ingenious landlord would find a happy expedient for his purse, if his tenants could live on the turnip as well as the potato. Like cattle these poor creatures seemed to be driven from one herb and root to another, using nettles, turnip-tops, chickweed, in their turn, and dying at last on these miserable substitutes. Many a child sitting in a muddy cabin has been interrogated, what she or he had to eat, " nothing but the turnip ma'am," sometimes the "turnip-top," and being asked when this was procured, sometimes the answer would be "yesterday, lady," or,

"when we can get it, ma'am."

Asenath Nicholson (1848)

DEAD ANIMALS

The following frightful fact will serve to show to what an extent the destitution of the people in this neighbourhood prevails. On Saturday week a horse, the properly of the Rev. Mr. Cawley of this town, died at Moygownagh, and shortly after the circumstances became known, some persons came to where the animal was lying, cut it up and took away the pieces for the purpose of eating them. Surely this single fact testifies more than ten thousand editorial articles could to the existence of the misery in which many of our unfortunate countrymen are now placed.

Tyrawly Herald (11-5-1848).

TRAGEDY AT MILL

We have received the following communication from our Ballinrobe correspondent: – A young girl named Bridget Glynn, aged sixteen years, was killed by the wheel of Mr. Mayne's mill, on Thursday last. The poor girl being (as thousands now are) starving went into the mill to try and get a little meal, and in endeavouring to get a handful of meal to eat, out of where it was grinding, her clothes got entangled in some way with the wheel and she was killed in an instant. Another human being sacrificed to the heartless and beggarly political economy of Lord John Russell and his effete and now constant eulogist the Liberator.

Mayo Constitution (8-12-1846).

Burials

People, weakened by hunger and fever, were unable to give proper burials to dead relatives and neighbours. Coffins could not be afforded and those who managed to carry their dead to the graveyard often did not have the strength to bury them. Workhouse dead were interred in mass graves. Some of the dead were buried where they died, in fields, on the side of the road, etc. Often, to avoid contracting fever, neighbours simply tumbled a victim's cabin around the body.

NO COFFINS IN CASTLEBAR

Another wretched woman died in Stabball last week, and for want of a coffin she lay on the damp floor of a hut for some days. A plate was laid on her face to keep the soot drops from it.

In Gallowshill another poor woman died from want; she remained from Sunday morning until Wednesday evening unburied, for want of a coffin, which was at length procured by the subscriptions of a few individuals.

Last week a female mendicant died at Coursepark, near Rathbane, in a house where she got shelter for the night. All efforts to procure a coffin for her proved fruitless, and a few days after her decease, far gone in decomposition, the body was laid on some wattles, tied with hay ropes, and in this horrible state was it borne through the streets of our town to the old church yard for interment.

It is not necessary for us to continue the soul-harrowing catalogue of deaths which daily and hourly occur in this town and neighbourhood from actual starvation, and upon which no inquests are held.

The Telegraph (10-2-1847).

CARRIED COFFIN FOUR MILES

We are daily witnessing horrid sights in this town (Castlebar) from starvation. A few days ago a poor young man died in Stabball, from want of food. After much time had been consumed in procuring a coffin, which was effected in three days after his death, we were horrified to behold the poor mother of the deceased carrying on her back the dead body by means of straw ropes at either end of the coffin: her only living companion being an old helpless woman. In this manner did the wretched parent convey the

inanimate remains of her son to the burying place at Turlough, a distance of nearly four miles. – Horrible.

The Telegraph (10-2-1847).

PILE OF STONES

DEATH FROM WANT – On Wednesday last the body of a poor woman was found dead in a field adjoining this town (Castlebar). A child belonging to the deceased had piled some stones round the body to protect it from the dogs and pigs.

The Telegraph (5-4-1847).

COFFINS VISIBLE IN LIEGUE AND KILMORE

For some time past the above burial grounds are in a most disgraceful and dangerous state, caused by the hurried and imperfect manner in which the bodies of several paupers, who died in the Workhouse, were committed to the earth. In some places the graves are so shallow that portions of the coffins are distinctly visible above ground without the slightest covering. At present we think the inhabitants of this town are exposed to quite enough of danger from fever and other Famine-generated diseases, without being exposed to further peril from the shameful state of two graveyards in their immediate vicinity. As nothing

can be more prejudicial to life than the exhalations arising from animal matter in process of decomposition, we are decidedly of opinion, that unless immediate steps be taken to remedy the evil of which we here complain, that when the Summer shall have set in, the fetid vapours arising from these half-covered graves and mingling with the surrounding atmosphere will produce a plague, causing, perhaps, in many instances, sudden death.

Tyrawly Herald (15-4-1847).

SHALLOW GRAVES

As the Summer advances the greater necessity for precaution as to health will become more and more apparent, it is this, therefore, that induces us to again call upon the inhabitants of Castlebar to adopt the necessary precaution of re-covering the numerous dead bodies lately interred in the old church yard. It is admitted on all hands that such is required – that the coffins are, in many instances, on a level with the surface of the field. What then, can hinder the spread of a horrible plague over this town and its vicinity? A subscription of eight or ten shillings, which would pay a few labourers to do the necessary work, may be the means of saving many valuable lives. May we hope to see this immediately set on foot. No time should be lost in doing it.

The Telegraph (12-5-1847).

CASTLEBAR WORKHOUSE DEAD

BURIAL OF WORKHOUSE PAUPERS: – Considerable annoyance and disgust has been felt by the inhabitants of this town, by the conveyance of the lifeless remains of paupers who may have died of fever and dysentery, through the principle streets; and, in many cases, the creatures carrying the remains have left down their burden to rest. We are certain the following resolution – entered into by the magistrates – will induce the present board to alter this regulation, and have the paupers buried in the graveyard attached to the workhouse:–

"Resolved – That it having been represented to the bench of magistrates this day that a very great grievance exists in the mode of carrying the bodies of paupers who have died of fever and other diseases, in the union workhouses. In many instances, the few persons employed on this duty are observed to loiter in the streets, and deposit the coffins on the ground for some time, which coffins are so imperfectly finished as to scarcely cover the bodies. We, therefore, request the vice-guardians will be pleased to regulate the burial of the dead with more order and decency, and, when practicable, to have them buried in the poorhouse ground that has been consecrat-ed, and not permit them, to the annoyance of the inhabitants, to be carried through this town.

THOMAS DILLON, M.D.,
WILLIAM KEARNEY.

29th July, 1847.

Mayo Constitution (3-8-1847).

SACK CLOTH

SHOCKING – On yesterday morning the inhabitants of this town were thrown into a state of consternation by beholding the revolting spectacle of a human dead body carried through the town on wattles, without a coffin, wrapped up in a piece of dirty sack cloth, bound round with two straw ropes – one round the neck and the other round the feet. Can there be anything more awful than this in a Christian country? Will those in the town and neighbourhood whom God has blessed with means, establish a coffin fund, in order that the inhabitants may not be shocked by a repetition of yesterday morning's proceedings?

The Telegraph (6-10-1847).

PAUPER BURIAL IN WESTPORT

The chapel bell tolled one morning early, when a respectable young woman was brought into the yard for interment. No bells tolled for the starving, they must have the "burial of an ass," or none at all. A young lad improved this opportunity while the gate was open, and carried in, a large sack on his back, which contained two brothers, one seventeen, the other a little boy, who had died by starvation. In one corner he dug, with his own emaciated feeble hands, a grave, and put them in, uncoffined, and covered them, while the clods were falling upon the coffin of the respectable young woman. I never witnessed a more stirring, striking contrast between civilised and savage life – Christianity and heathenism – wealth for the mockery of death, with all its trappings and ceremonies – the mockery of pompous funerals, and their black retinue. This poor boy unheeded had staid in the dark cabin with those dead brothers, not even getting admittance into the gate, till some respectable one should want a burial; then he might follow this procession at a suitable distance, with two dead brothers upon his back, and put them in with his own hands, with none to compassionate him!

Asenath Nicholson (1847).

WATTLES

AWFULLY HORRIBLE: – Within the last week numbers of dead bodies have passed our Office, for interment in the Old Church yard, borne on wattles, WITHOUT COFFINS! One of those bodies, that of a full grown person, was carried by women!

The Telegraph (5-4-1848).

CLEARING OUT A POOR HOUSE

At one o'clock on Sunday four dead bodies were carried abreast through this town, from the workhouse, for interment. We have heard that it is usual with the Master to hold over the bodies in the dead cell until he has a good batch to send through the town. This displays very little decency on his part, or respect for the feeling of the inhabitants, so heavily taxed to support him in his situation.

The Telegraph (19-4-1848).

Evictions

As the Famine progressed, increasing numbers of smallholders fell into arrears with rent. Some landlords were also in financial difficulty, but continued to alleviate distress among their tenantry. Others used the Famine as an opportunity to clear their lands of several small holdings and turn them into larger and more lucrative units.

CLANMORRIS LANDS, BALLYGLASS

On Friday last at an early hour, Counsellor White, accompanied by three bailiffs from Castlebar, on two post cars, proceeded to the neighbourhood of Ballyglass, to execute decrees for rent obtained by him at the suit of the late Lord Clanmorris. The bailiffs of the learned gentleman succeeded in making some seizures, whereupon a mob of between two and three-hundred country people rushed upon them and effected a rescue. They then attacked Mr. White and his men with stones and other missiles, nor did they stay their brutal work until they left the learned gentleman for dead on the road. His head is shockingly lacerated with stone wounds: his body, arms and thighs are bruised and blackened to a horrible degree. They afterwards opened his port mantua and took out all his papers which they destroyed, among which were some money orders and bank cheques of much value. The learned gentleman now lies at the residence of the Rev. Mr. Green, Protestant Minister, Mayo, where he is attended by Dr. Browne of Balla, and where he is visited by the gentry of the neighbourhood, who deeply commiserate with him on the unfortunate event which had well nigh deprived him of existence.

The Telegraph (7-9-1848).

EVICTED AND IMPRISONED

Last week a poor man named Devir died in the Mayo Prison under very peculiar circumstances. It appears he owed a certain western Landlord a trifling debt. – say nine shillings! for which a decree was obtained, by virtue of which the poor man was dragged from his family and cast into prison! His wife and children sought relief from the Poor Law officials, and were taken into the workhouse in Castlebar. Banished from house and home by would-be-thought Christians! For NINE SHILLINGS! the wretched man sickened and died. After his decease the officers of the prison tied up his old clothes and had them conveyed to the poor widow at the workhouse! The reader can more easily imagine than we can describe, the feelings of the widowed wife and orphan children, when, for a husband and father, they were presented with his old wearables after his death! The unfortunate woman carried the cherished garments into the field adjoining the workhouse; and there gave vent to the sorrow which wrecked her grieved and bursting heart.

The Telegraph (12-7-1848).

An eviction scene.

SIR ROGER PALMER

During the last fortnight the "Crowbar Brigade" of Sir Roger Palmer, Bart., have been busily employed in the district of Islandeady, Glenisland, etc., in "levelling" the houses of the worthy Baronet's tenantry and hunting the occupants to seek shelter or DEATH! beneath the hedges, clefts of rocks, and in peat banks. No mercy was displayed towards any one of the besieged: one man, in the convulsive pangs of death, was thrown out into the open air, and in an hour or two after, we learn, death put an end to his miserable existence. While the cold messenger was hastening the soul of the poor outcast before its heavenly Judge the fiends of this earth were zealously engaged in pulling down the house from which they dragged him forth in the throes of death! We here annex the names of some of those whose houses have been levelled, with the number of each family and the townland:–

Names	Residence	Family	Remarks.
Patt Shaughnessy	Drimnaganean	10	
Patt Moylet	ditto	6	
James Moran	ditto	10	
Sally Chambers	ditto	5	Widow
Patt Kelly	ditto	2	Orphans
Patt Gallagher	ditto	4	
Patt Murray	ditto	5	
Bridget Gallagher	ditto	7	Widow
Daniel Gallagher	ditto	5	Orphans
Owen McEllin	ditto	6	
Bridget Burke	ditto	4	Widow
Michael Kelly	ditto	3	
John Kane	ditto	4	
Patt Kane	Monageerane	4	
Celia Hesten	ditto	3	Widow
Mary Hesten	ditto	5	Widow
Mary Berry	ditto	4	Widow
Bridget Gallagher	ditto	2	Widow
Peggy Kirby	ditto	2	Widow
Mary Callaghan	ditto	5	Widow
Daniel Murry	ditto	5	
Michael Kirby	ditto	8	
John Fennaghty	ditto	8	
Catherine Lally	ditto	5	Widow
Bridget Bourke	ditto	4	Widow
William Mulroy	ditto	7	
Judy Heston	ditto	2	Widow
Michael Joyce	ditto	3	
Bryan McHugh	Kelhale	3	
Denis Shiel	ditto	9	
James Shiel	ditto	5	
Patt Kelly	ditto	6	
Michael Philbin	ditto	3	
Sally Langan	ditto	5	Widow
Nancy Reily	ditto	3	Widow
Patt Naven	ditto	6	
Peter Barrett	ditto	6	
Francis Sherins	ditto	2	

The Telegraph (5-9-1849).

MANULLA

The following families were evicted on the 26th inst., from the townland of Ruslahan (the property of Henry S. Jones, Esq., Mountjoy Square, Dublin) in the Parish and Electoral Division of Drum, and Union of Castlebar, viz: – James Foster; James Dowd, Thomas Kerigan, James Kerigan; John Dowd, Richard Barrett, James Kennedy, Pat McDonnell, James Killilea, in fever; Michael Moran, in fever; Daniel Surdival, Hubert Bourke. All these are destitute – no provision made for them by the Guardians or their subalterns, as the law directs – or does the law make any provision for such persons? The number in each family vary from five to nine.

The Telegraph (7-11-1848).

NEWPORT

NEWPORT and its vicinity presented a variety of exciting scenes: here in this pretty town, families of tolerable comfort declined step by step, till many who would have outlived the common changes of life could not maintain their standing in this hour of trial.

Sir Richard O'Donnell is the landlord in possession of most of the land there, and his "driver," like others akin to him, does strange things to the tenants, quite unknown to the landlord, who has been called humane.

But this fearless "driver" throws, or causes to be thrown down, cabin after cabin, and sometimes whole villages, of which it is said the landlord was entirely ignorant, but the pitiless storm heeded not that, and the poor starved exiles pleading that the cabin might be left a little longer, have not pity, their pot and even the cloak, which is the peasant women's all by night and by day, has often been torn from her emaciated limbs, and sold at auction. Perhaps in no instance does the oppression of the poor, and the sighing of the needy come before the mind so vividly, as when going over the places made desolate by the Famine, to see the tumbled cabins, with the poor hapless inmates, who had for years sat around their turf fire, and ate their potato together, now lingering and oftimes wailing in despair, their ragged barefooted little ones clinging about them, one on the back of the weeping mother, and the father looking in silent despair, while a part of them are scraping among the rubbish to gather some little relic of mutual attachment – (for the poor, reader, have their tender remembrances) – then, in a flock, take their solitary, their pathless way to seek some rock or ditch, to encamp supperless for the night, without either a covering for the head or the feet, with not the remnant of a blanket to spread over them in the ditch, where they must crawl. Are these solitary cases? Happy would it be were it so; but village upon village, and company after company have I seen; and one magistrate who was travelling informed me that at nightfall the preceding day, he found a company who had gathered a few sticks and fastened them into the ditch, and spread over what miserable rags they could collect (for the rain was fast pouring), and under these more than two hundred men, women and children, were to crawl for the night. He alighted from his car, and counted more than two-hundred; they had all that day been driven out, and not ONE pound of any kind of food was in the whole encampment!

Asenath Nicholson (1848).

ISLANDEADY

HOUSE-LEVELLING – Near the half-way house, Westport road, on the estate of Sir Roger Palmer, Bart., Tom (the brother of George! desirous of emulating

that kind and gentle agent in all his acts) on Wednesday last, assisted by the crowbar invincibles, pulled down several houses, and drove forth the fortunate inmates to sleep in the adjoining fields. On Thursday we witnessed the wretched creatures endeavouring to root out the timber of the houses, with the intention of construct-ing some sort of sheds to screen their children from the heavy rain falling at the time. On Wednesday night there was a deluge of rain, the severity of which those poor creatures were exposed to in the open fields. Unfortunately for them, the pitiless pelting storm has continued ever since, and if they have survived its severity they must be more than human beings. Happy tenantry! blessed with such kind hearted agents,

whose desire manifestly is to give them as much fresh air as possible - and, to facilitate their procurement of food, send them forth to "EAT GRASS!"

The Telegraph (5-7-1848).

SIR ROGER PALMER'S ERRIS LANDS

HOUSE LEVELLING – On Thursday last, as we were returning from Belmullet, our feelings were shocked by witnessing several houses on the estate of Sir Roger Palmer under the process of being demolished and their unfortunate inmates cast forth on the world. Such conduct, at any time, should be considered

An evicted family seeks refuge in a ditch.

as heartless, but at present, when want and death are decimating the poor people we look upon it as monstrous, and the promoters of it less humanised than savages.

Tyrawly Herald (7-9-1848).

GEORGE BINGHAM, 3rd EARL OF LUCAN

Lord Lucan has 60,570 acres in Mayo, part of it around Castlebar, where his substantial old house stands; part of it at Cloona Castle, near Ballinrobe. From several parishes extensive evictions were made from 1846 to 1850; throwing together the smaller holdings, several large grazing and a few considerable tillage farms were made. Lord Lucan, in his terse, incisive style, asserted that "he would not breed paupers to pay priests." With a sort of military despotism, he has endeavoured personally to rule his estates. Hurried visits to Mayo have not, however, always furnished him with sound information as to agricultural or social difficulties; his local lieutenants have had small authority; their opinions have often been hastily set aside; little has been done to develop either Castlebar, the villages on the estate, or the agriculture of the country.

(Finlay Dun: "Landlords and Tenants in Ireland" – 1881).

Earl of Lucan *(From the Wynne Collection).*

KILMACLASSER – MORE LANDLORDISM IN MAYO

TO THE EDITOR OF THE MAYO TELEGRAPH.

Half-Parish of Kilmaclasser, Westport, June 24, 1848.

Sir – I beg leave to enclose you a correct list of the houses that have been demolished and the persons evicted within the last three weeks in this parish – all on the property of the Right Hon. the Earl of Lucan: for be it known to all whom it may concern, that His Lordship has the enviable distinction of being hitherto the only Gerrardiser in the electoral division of Kilmaclasser. In the course of a few days you shall have a list of the depopulations in the Kilmeena divisions. I may add, that severals of those whose houses have been levelled by that pink of landlords, the Earl of Lucan, had actually made fine tillage; but, alas! of them it may be well said, "Sic vos non vobis,' – they have sown, but others shall reap.

Yours truly,
THOMAS HARDIMAN.

NUMBER OF HOUSES LEVELLED IN KILTRANE

Martin Cain, having 10 in family, living in Knockmenard.
John Cain, having 6 in family, do. do.
Thomas Cain, having 2 in family, living in Kiltrane.
George O'Brien, having 2 in family, living in Knockmenard.
Widow Reilly, having 1 in family, living in Michael O'Brien's.
John Moran, having 10 in family, living in a shed.
Daniel McGreal's orphans, 4 in family, living in Knockbee.
Widow Cusack, having 2 in family, living in Patt McLoughlin's.
John Sheridan, having 6 in family, living in a shed.
Thomas Cusack, having 6 in family, living at Louisburgh.
Hugh Cain, having 6 in family, living in Fahy.
Widow Wehan, having 5 in family, living in a shed.

AUGHAGOWLMORE

Sarah Scanlan, having 2 in family, living in a neighbour's house.
Henry Kearny, having 4 in family, do., do.
Widow Cusack, having 3 in family, do., do.
John Horan, having 3 in family, gone to England.
John Heraghty, having 3 in family, do., do.

AUGHAGOWLABEG

Pat Carney, having 2 in family – wife living in a neighbouring house.

DRIMULRA

Pat Gannon, having 4 in family, gone to neighbouring house.
Patt Quinn, having 8 in family, living in a shed of his own.
Terence Quinn, having 4 in family, do., do.
Austin McGreal, having 6 in family, do., do.
John Quinn, having 5 in family, do., do.
Edward Gibbons, having 4 in family, do., do.
John McGreal, having 3 in family, do., do.
Michael Salmon, having 5 in family, do., do.
Widow Lackey (McGreal), 6 in family, do., do.
Anthony Moran, having 3 in family, do., do.
Widow Salmon, living in a shed.

The Telegraph (5-7-1848).

Emigration

For many, emigration became a means of escaping the hunger. Many departed for England, America and Australia, some from ports in Mayo. Most emigrants were forced to avail of the cheapest passages where conditions aboard vessels were atrocious, with overcrowding and poor sanitation. Emigrants often had to provide their own food and eat and sleep on their allocation of a few square feet of timber. Water was often in short supply. In such conditions fever spread and many died at sea.

EMBARKING AT BELMULLET

EMIGRATION – We cheerfully publish the following, forwarded to us by our valued Correspondent at Belmullet:–

"On the morning of the 16th instant the small steamer, Unity, from Sligo, arrived here to convey the Erris emigrants, bound for America, to join the passengers at Sligo. On the quay it was really frightful to hear, and see, those creatures bewailing their hard fate in being obliged to leave their native land, and to separate from all they held dear on earth, their friends and relatives – the husband from his wife – the father from his children – the son from his mother – brothers from sisters, and daughters from mothers. I had conversed with many of them whom I thought were in comfortable circumstances, but alas! their tale was truly doleful and lamentable, stating that they were in daily expectation of relief or employment from the Government, since their stock of potatoes had perished by the frightful disease, but they at length fully understood the procrastination of their Rulers – now that they were going to give them coercion as a substitute for food or employment, and knowing that whatever effects they possessed would be swallowed up by the next rent they determined on the present course to save themselves and families from utter ruin. They were all Repealers - and, the tears of sorrow which they shed on the shore of their dear loved biland home I shall never forget, as the Belmullet Temperance Band played for them the National airs of their country.

Previous to their embarkation they were several times heard to exclaim, "that the land of liberty might afford them an opportunity of remembering the land of Coercion." The poor fellows boasted "that they were free, as they owed no debt." As for rent, of course, the Landlord's Agents were more assiduous this season than at any other, by being before hand, in order to secure themselves, whatever might become of the people's food. I do believe that there are not ten pounds due for rent in all Erris this day. My ears thrill with the frightful cries of separating friends while I write. I could give particulars more calamitous of the creatures who are not so fortunate as to commend the means of taking them to America, and whose last meal of potatoes and last penny are now exhausted."

The Telegraph (22-4-1846).

HORRIFIC VOYAGE OF THE ELIZABETH AND SARA

TO THE EDITOR OF THE MONTREAL HERALD

Quebec, 22nd August, 1846.

Sir – The suffering which we have undergone, in our late voyage across the Atlantic, and our desire to save others from experiencing similar treatment, induces us to address this letter to you; and to request that you will publish it. We deem it, Sir, a duty that we owe to our fellow

A priest blesses departing emigrants.

AT WESTPORT,
FOR PHILADELPHIA,
TO SAIL ABOUT 10th OCTOBER,

THE SPLENDID FIRST-CLASS,

Coppered and Copper-fastened, British Built Ship,

GREAT BRITAIN,

BURTHEN, 600 TONS,

R. WILSON, COMMANDER.

THIS well known, fast-sailing Ship is now discharging her Cargo of Indian Corn at Westport.

She will be fitted up with every attention to the comfort of Passengers, who will receive the usual allowance of Provisions and Water during the passage.

Application to be made to Captain WILSON, on board ; or at the Office of

JOHN REID, Jun., & CO.,
Ship Agents, Westport Quay.

Westport, 21st September, 1848.

A typical advertisment dated, Autumn, 1848.

countrymen – many of whom, yearly seek a home upon the shores of Canada – to expose the nefarious stratagems and deceits, and their consequences, that were practised upon us, by Hugh Leighton, Ship-broker, of Sligo, Hugh Simpson, his clerk, and John Reilly, merchant, of Belmullet, who used every means in their power, to induce us to embark, at Killala, on board the "Elizabeth and Sarah," whereof A. Simpson was master. Circulars were sent round by Reilly, towards the latter end of April, which stated to us that he had a vessel, which would sail from Killala on the first of May, for this Port. There being no time to lose we sold, at a sacrifice, what few effects we possessed, paid our deposits of twenty shillings each, and immediately proceeded to Killala. But, Sir, who can imagine the feelings of anguish and disappointment which filled our breasts, on arriving there, to find no vessel.

There we were, without even a roof to protect us from the changes of the weather, most of us having resided at a distance of from 30 to 40 miles from that place, and having there conveyed ourselves and families at a considerable expense; in this state we were obliged to return, not to our homes - they were in the hands of strangers – but to beg a scanty shelter from our former neighbours. After a while we were again informed, by the above-named persons, that the vessel had arrived at Killala, and that should we not reach that place by the 14th of May, we would forfeit our deposits. This time, indeed, we found the vessel in Port, but she was far from being ready for sea; and we received for answer to our eager enquiries, that she would sail in a day or two; in the mean time we were obliged to live in Boarding Houses, the expense of which consumed our all, being the proceeds of what

we had sold to enable us to make a start in America. Day after day flew by, a week elapsed, but still no signs of departure, till, finally, on the 26th day of May, we weighed anchor, and bid adieu to the shores of our native land.

And now, Sir, commences a tale of misery and suffering which, we hope to God, none of our fellow mortals may ever experience. Before leaving Killala, Hugh Leighton, Hugh Simpson and Thomas Townley gave us to understand that each berth was occupied by six persons, and that the number of passengers was not to exceed 216; after we had sailed, however, it was found that we numbered 280 souls, and that instead of there being 47 berths, as there should have been for this number of persons, there were 36 in all, 4 of which were afterwards occupied by the crew; so that there remained but 32 for the accommodation of the passengers, which being totally insufficient for our number, many of us were obliged to sleep on the floor. Two quarts of water per day, was the most allowed to each passenger; nor was bread or oatmeal ever served out to us, as stated in our passage tickets; and which, by law, the master was bound to have given us. After having been out twenty-one days the master informed us, that we were on the Banks of Newfoundland; whereupon many of the passengers wasted their provisions, believing that they were close to port; we did not reach Newfoundland for twenty-four days after this, and instead of finding ourselves on the South side, we were on the North; we had to make the circuit of the Island of Newfoundland to gain the Gulf of St. Lawrence, but before doing this, the Mate, Jeremiah Tindal (the Captain being sick, and unable to attend to his duties), ran us ashore on the Island of St. Peter to the South of Newfoundland, thinking at the time, it was St. Paul's Island; we were then in a most deplorable state, living upon short allowance, and many of us without any; our pittance of water was both gluey and putrid; disease and pestilence broke out among us and carried off many of our fellow passengers in its grasp. In this state of things, we succeeded in getting off the reef, luckily without much inquiry; our Captain who, for many days past, had been at death's door, now breathed his last, and several more of the passengers likewise yielded up their souls to him who created them. Their bodies were, of course, immediately committed to the deep; but the Mate, as if to add to our misery, notwithstanding our most urgent requests to the contrary, persisted in keeping the body of the Captain. For thirteen long days (at the end of which time we reached Basque Island), the body lay upon the quarter deck in a most horrid, disgusting state of decomposition, thereby engendering the pestilence among us to a fearful extent, insomuch that twenty-two souls had, by this time, perished.

Shortly after leaving the reef at St. Peter's Island, we fell in with a vessel, and it was with the utmost difficulty that we induced the Mate to heave-to, in hopes of obtaining a fresh supply of water and provisions, both of which he got, and sold the latter to us at most exorbitant prices; a few days after this we met another vessel, but the cruel Mate would not heave to – no – the unfeeling man continued his course, notwithstanding the heart-rending cries of men, women and children, who clung to his knees in the agony of their despair. At Basque Island we received much attention from a Mr. Webb, Mate of the Liverpool, wrecked at that Island, and whose disinterested kindness, while it never can be forgotten by us, we would wish to be particularly noticed, as it might be serviceable to him in obtaining his promotion, which he well deserves. There, Sir, we would have laid till our ship had become a charnel house, and we had no longer been numbered among the living, had it not been for the promptitude and decision of the Government Emigrant Agent here, in despatching a steamboat to our assistance, as he was informed of our melancholy situation; for this act, he will ever have our most earnest prayers rising to the mercy seat of God beseeching him that he will forever bless both him and his.

On the 72nd day after our departure from Killala, we dropped anchor at Grosse Isle, where we were kindly and hospitably treated by Dr. Douglas, the Medical Superintendent, as also by Mr. Cullingford, who was in charge of the sick; here seven more of our fellow passengers died, and many still remain there in a very precarious state.

We are, Sir,
Your obedient servants
*(Signed on behalf of their
fellow passengers)*,

JOHN LAVAL,
Late of the parish of Kilmore;

JOHN STEPHENS,
Late of the Parish of Westport;

JAMES JOYCE,
Late of the Parish of Laumore
(County Mayo),

Tyrawly Herald (24-9-1846).

STATEMENT OF THE NUMBER OF EMIGRANTS

Which have arrived at the Port of New York, for the present year, from January to September, inclusive.

From:

Ireland	72,896
Germany	40,731
England	17,223
Scotland	4,974
France	2,007
Holland	1,374
Switzerland	1,243
Norway	4,206
Wales	899
West Indies	335
Spain	225
Italy	241
Sweden	113
Poland	53
Denmark	33
Portugal	35
South America	21
Russia	11
Mexico	7
Belgium	4
China	1

143,632

Mayo Constitution (31-10-1848)

Emigrants crowded in the hold.

AMERICAN
EMIGRATION OFFICE,

96, *WATERLOO ROAD, LIVERPOOL.*

THE Subscribers continue to despatch first-class Packets to NEW YORK, BOSTON, QUEBEC, MONTREAL, PHILADELPHIA, NEW ORLEANS, and ST. JOHN'S, N.B.

FOR NEW YORK,
The favourite Packet-ships,
Tons,
HOTTINGUER, Captain BURSLEY.. 1150 tons....6th Jan.

Parties residing at a distance may have every information by letter, and the best disengaged berths secured by sending deposits of 1l for each Passenger to
GEORGE RIPPARD and SON.
Or to JOHN FLANAGAN,
General Emigration Agent, Newport, Mayo.
. Each week in succession, and independent of the Monthly Packets, First Class Vessels are despatched by Messrs RIPPARD to the principal American ports.
LOCAL AGENTS.
Mr ALEXANDER BOLE, Castlebar, Mr PETER O'FLANAGAN, Tuam; Mr ADAM NEALE, Ballinrobe; Mr THOMAS HUGHES, Turin Castle, Kilmain; Mr CLAUDIUS NIXON, Ballina; Mr. FRANCIS O'DONNELL, Knockmore, Ballyglass; Mr ARTHUR ROSS, Belmullet; Mr LAWRENCE GEOGHAN, High-sreet, Galway; Mr MICHAEL JACKSON Killala

A typical advertisement dated, Autumn, 1848.

ENCOURAGEMENT TO EMIGRATION

Australia – Extract, September, 1846 –

"The things we are in greater want of is labour. We are giving 35l. a year for a man and his wife, and 25l. a year for shepherds, besides rations, which consist of 10 lbs. of flour, 12 lbs. of beef, 2 lbs. of sugar, and three-quarter lbs. of tea per week, and a house to live in, by no means hard work. We have a great many working men earning from 30s. to 12s. per week."

Tyrawly Herald (8-14-1847).

ALL CLASSES EMIGRATING

The spirit of emigration is quite prevalent in this town and neighbourhood. Within the last few days about thirty departed hence to seek, in a foreign clime, that independence, which they were fast losing in their native land, and we have reason to believe that many more are preparing to follow. The class of persons emigrating belong entirely to those individuals who formed the bone and sinew of the country. Substantial farmers, and men engaged in industrious pursuits, who behold themselves threatened with destitution by means of the Famine and the operation of the Poor Law, are the persons that are wending their way to other lands in order to rescue themselves and their families from the grasp of poverty. None but those whose circumstances prevent them from going are remaining at home. The consequences, likely to arise from this course of proceeding, must be easily foreseen. In a short time we shall have none but paupers in the country, and then cannot it be asked how will poor rates, county cess, and other taxes be paid up? Let squalid poverty be personified and that respectable personage can answer the question.

Tyrawly Herald (9-11-1848).

WORKHOUSE EMIGRANTS

The vice-guardians of this union have made preparation for the emigration of 19 of the best conducted female inmates of the Castlebar workhouse, who are to proceed to Dublin on Thursday next per Bianconi's car. We understand that a similar number are about being sent from Westport, Ballinrobe, and Ballina workhouses. These girls are well supplied with clothing and other necessaries, all at the expense of the respective unions.

Mayo Constitution (18-9-1849).

The packet ship "Cornelius Grinnell"

Population Decline

Over the period 1841-1851, the population of Ireland fell from 8,175,124, the highest recorded, to 6,55,385.
The overall decline was 20%, but, in some counties it was higher. The population of County Mayo fell by
29%, from 388,887 to 274,830, due to deaths and emigration. Emigration became a long-term legacy
of the Famine, with each successive census showing a decline in population which
reached a low of 109,525 in 1971.

Parish	Population		Houses		Parish	Population		Houses	
	1841	1851	1841	1851		1841	1851	1841	1851
Achill	6,392	4,950	1,387	956	Castlemore	2,944	2,831	520	508
Addergoole	7,379	5,085	1,313	949	Cong	5,359	3,839	999	758
Aghagower	12,235	6,511	2,298	1,302	Crossboyne	6,702	4,963	1,195	953
Aghamore	7,675	6,097	1,427	1,241	Crossmolina	12,221	7,236	2,219	1,278
Aglish	10,464	9,135	1,835	1,196	Doonfeeny	4,819	2,720	865	491
Annagh	7,904	6,105	1,477	1,194	Drum	4,127	2,732	758	548
Ardagh	2,621	1,497	463	263	Inishbofin	1,612	1,047	288	196
Attymass	3,435	2,431	651	463	Islandeady	8,463	4,699	1,556	921
Balla	1,934	1,272	331	224	Kilbeagh	9,963	9,733	1,784	1,774
Ballinchalla	1,722	1,420	311	275	Kilbelfad	3,681	2,296	629	423
Ballinrobe	10,115	9,326	1,884	1,303	Kilbride	1,963	1,144	329	193
Ballintober	7,199	3,438	1,355	672	Kilcolman				
Ballyheane	4,032	1,987	798	405	(Claremorris)	9,451	7,421	1,670	1,323
Ballynahaglish	5,397	3,393	956	664	Kilcolman (Costello				
Ballyovey	4,505	3,073	792	590	– Part)	4,365	4,151	754	717
Balysakeery	6,034	2,951	1,068	571	Kilcommon	7,456	5,255	1,285	952
Bekan	5,589	4,724	1,053	886	Kilcommon				
Bohola	4,301	2,907	737	561	(Erris)	17,000	12,253	2,935	2,079
Breaghwy	2,452	1,136	456	218	Kilconduff	7,072	6,909	1,287	1,140
Burrishcarra	1,681	913	296	162	Kilcummin	2,791	1,552	500	293
Burrishoole	11,942	7,528	2,217	1,254	Kildacommoge	3,923	2,234	710	420

A deserted village.

The effects of the Famine:
this map shows the percentage
population decline per county
between 1841 and 1851.

DONEGAL
-14

DERRY
-14

-9
ANTRIM

Belfast
City
+24

TYRONE
-18

-26
FERMANAGH

-16
ARMAGH

DOWN
-11

SLIGO
-29

LEITRIM
-28

MONAGHAN
-29

MAYO
-29

CAVAN
-28

LOUTH
-16

ROSCOMMON
-32

-29
LONGFORD
-21
WESTMEATH

MEATH
-23

+5

DUBLIN
Dublin
City
+11

GALWAY
-27

KING'S
OFFALY

KILDARE
-16

-23

-27
QUEEN'S
LAOIS

WICKLOW
-22

CLARE
-26

-21
CARLOW

TIPPERARY

KILKENNY

LIMERICK
-21

-24

-22

WEXFORD
-11

WATERFORD
-16

KERRY
-19

CORK
-24

Parish	Population		Houses	
	1841	1851	1841	1851
Kilfian	5,040	3,348	1,094	589
Kilgarvan	4,158	3,194	785	580
Kilgeever	12,573	6,892	2,309	1,263
Killala	3,253	2,919	593	400
Killasser	6,962	4,852	1,240	949
Killedan	6,410	5,158	1,168	1,047
Kilmacclasser	3,548	1,614	630	315
Kilmainebeg	1,491	895	255	174
Kilmainemore	4,877	3,293	898	645
Kilmeena	7,876	5,108	1,398	929
Kilmolara	1,296	864	243	180
Kilmore (Erris)	9,428	7,379	1,720	1,106
Kilmoremoy	7,028	6,393	1,318	1,163
Kilmovee	5,844	5,882	1,095	1,120
Kilturra (Part)	1,350	1,023	259	200
Kilvine	2,236	1,697	392	308
Knock	3,374	3,174	616	600
Lackan	2,943	1,176	511	207
Manulla	2,336	1,387	404	241
Mayo	4,179	2,379	751	434
Meelick	3,915	2,692	680	521
Moorgagagh	627	294	112	54
Oughaval	13,441	13,282	2,385	1,741
Rathreagh	1,664	790	287	146
Robeen	3,544	2,522	638	505
Rosslee	1,283	694	216	143
Shrule	5,087	3,004	876	565
Tagheen	3,084	2,051	582	389
Templemore	4,251	2,387	770	434
Templemurry	1,291	514	242	83
Toomore	3,744	2,498	707	500
Touaghty	1,297	884	232	156
Turlough	7,430	4,516	1,369	893
TOTAL	388,887	274,830	70,542	49,073

Lord Lucan in later years (Wynne Collection).

AGHADRINAGH TOWNLAND

(based on the Ordnance Survey, by permission of the Government – Permit No.: 6407).

Before: from Ordnance Survey (1839).

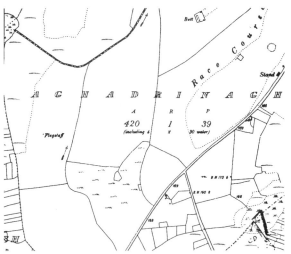

After: from Ordnance Survey (1900).

Reform

In 1879 Michael Davitt, who was born at Straide in County Mayo, founded the Land League. This mass movement campaigned for reform of land legislation which eventually transformed tenant farmers into owners of the land.

"Straide was my birthplace, and almost my first-remembered experience of my own life and of the existence of landlordism was our eviction in 1852, when I was about five years of age. That eviction and the privations of the preceding Famine years, the story of the starving peasantry of Mayo, of the deaths from hunger – and the coffinless graves on the roadside – everywhere a hole could be dug for the slaves who died because of 'God's providence' – all this was the political food seasoned with a mother's tears over unmerited sorrows and sufferings which had fed my mind in another land, a teaching which lost none of its force or directness by being imparted in the Gaelic tongue, which was almost always spoken in our Lancashire home."

Michael Davitt,

"The Fall of Feudalism in Ireland" 1904.

Acknowledgements

The Connaught Telegraph, Castlebar.

The Western People, Ballina.

The Wynne Family, Castlebar.

Forde Photography, Newbrook, Claremorris.

Ordnance Survey, Dublin.